Sergeant Lawrence

Sergeant Lawrence

With the 40th Regt. of Foot in
South America, the Peninsular War
& at Waterloo

William Lawrence

LEONAUR

Sergeant Lawrence: with the 40th Regt. of Foot in South America, the Peninsular War & at Waterloo
by William Lawrence

Published by Leonaur Ltd

ISBN: 978-1-84677-388-4 (hardcover)
ISBN: 978-1-84677-387-7 (softcover)

http://www.leonaur.com

Publisher's Note

The opinions expressed in this book are those of the author
and are not necessarily those of the publisher.

Contents

Preface	7
Early Adventures	11
I Join the Fortieth Regiment	16
South America: the River Plate Expedition	20
Colonia	26
Buenos Ayres	32
The Peninsula: the Battle of Vimeira	36
The Battle of Talavera	42
The Battle of Busaco	47
The Lines of Torres Vedras	52
Ordered to Badajoz	59
Badajoz & Albuera	65
Ciudad Rodrigo	70
The Forlorn Hope	77
I Make Corporal	86
Battle of Vittoria	93
Advance to the Pyrenees	101
I am Promoted to Sergeant	108
San Sebastian & Nivelle	117
Advance to Orthes	122
The End of the War	129
To America & Back	135
Waterloo	141
Advance to Paris	150
The March to Calais	157
The New Set of Colours	161
Studland	169

Preface

Sergeant William Lawrence died at Studland in Dorsetshire in the year 1867, bequeathing the manuscript of the accompanying autobiography to the family one of whose members now submits it to the notice of the public. Circumstances, which perhaps may be too often interpreted as really meaning an unfortunate tendency to procrastination, have hitherto prevented it being put into shape with a view to publication. One thing after another has intervened, and the work has been passed on from hand to hand, until after these long years a final effort has been made, and the self-imposed task completed.

The book is simply sent forth on its own merits in the hope that there are yet some, if not indeed many whose hearts are never weary of the tales of England's glory in the past, and seek to find in them reason why that glory should be perpetuated. Many an account have we already had of the victories of the Peninsula and Waterloo, and this but adds one more to the list: though perhaps it may be regarded in somewhat of a supplementary light, as treating of the campaigns neither from an entirely outside and *soi-disant* unprejudiced standpoint, nor with the advantages possessed by one who may have had access to the councils of the authorities, but as they were seen by one who came and went and did as he was told, and was as it were nothing more than a single factor in the great military machine that won our country those battles of which she has so much right to be proud. What criticisms of the conduct of the war our veteran occasionally does indulge in are of course chiefly founded on the camp gossip current at the time, and in reading them it must always be borne in mind that events at the moment of their happening often do not present the same appearance as when viewed from the calmer security of after years, and they must be judged accordingly.

As to the style. Lawrence, though he never betrayed the fact to the authorities during his whole military career, being possessed of a wonderful aptitude for mental calculation, and always contriving to get some assistance in concealing his deficiency when his official duties necessitated his doing so, and though he has carefully avoided all direct allusion to it in this work itself, never learnt to write, and the first form in which his history was committed to paper was from dictation. The person who took down the words as he spoke them, one of his fellow-servants, was but imperfectly educated himself, so that it may be imagined that the result of the narrative of one illiterate person being written down by another was that the style was not likely to aspire to any very high degree of literary merit. Still, to preserve the peculiar character of the book, it has been thought better to leave it as far as possible in its original shape: some emendations have perforce had to be made to render it actually intelligible—for instance, in the original manuscript there is scarcely any punctuation from beginning to end, with the exception of at those places where the amanuensis evidently left off his day's work; but the language, with its occasional half-flights into a poetry of about the standard of an Eton boy's verses, its crude moralizing, and. imperfect applications of old proverbs and fables, has not been altered, nor, so far as there can be said to be one, has the method. It is trusted, therefore, that, remembering that the main object in the editor's mind has been to let the venerable hero tell his story in exactly his own words so far as his meaning can be thereby made, out, no one will take any unnecessary pains to count up how often the words "likewise" and "proceed" are repeated in these pages, or to point out that the general style of the book combines those of Tacitus, Cæsar's Commentaries, and the Journeyings of the Israelites. Nor, it is to be hoped, will any one be too severe in his comments on the fact that to the mind of a man in Lawrence's position the obtaining of a pair of boots was apparently quite as important an event as the storming of Badajoz, or the finding of a sack with a ham and a couple of fowls in it as the winning of the battle of Waterloo.

Interesting perhaps the book will prove as giving some of the details of what our soldiers had to undergo in those old times of war. Hardships they now have to endure, and endure them they do well, but all must be thankful to know that they are far better off than their forefathers; who, unsuitably clad, half starved, and with their commissariat such even as it was disgracefully mismanaged, and yet forbidden very often under pain of death to pick up what they could for themselves, submitted on the shortest notice to punishments which would nowadays call forth the indignant protests of hosts of newspaper correspondents; and still in spite of all fought stubbornly through every obstacle till they had gained the objects for which they had been sent out. What wonder can there be that under all these circumstances we should find our hero somewhat hardened in his estimate of human sympathies, and not altogether disinclined to view everything, whether it concerned life or death, or marriage, or parting or meeting, all in one phlegmatic way, as occurring as a matter of course? What ought to strike us as more curious is that he was only reduced to that level of intellect where he thought even that much of anything at all besides his actual eating, drinking, and sleeping.

But to go on further would be to depart from the original intention of letting the book speak for itself. To conclude therefore there is much to wade through, though it is all more or less relevant to the progress of the story, some readers may like one part and some may prefer another; and if the pruning-hook had once been introduced it would have been difficult to decide what to leave and what to take, or whether it would not be better to publish another volume of the things pruned, since it had been determined to publish at all. But if the reader will accomplish the wading to the end, there will he find summed up in one simple paragraph the autobiographer's own ideas about the merits of his work. May it be received in the same spirit as it is sent forth!

CHAPTER 1

Early Adventures

As I have been asked to furnish as complete an account as I am able of my own life, and it is usual when people undertake to do so to start at as early a period as possible, I will begin with my parentage. My father and mother were of humble means, living in the village of Bryant's Piddle, in the county of Dorset. My father had been formerly a small farmer on his own account in the same village, but having a large and hungry family to provide for, he became reduced in circumstances, and was obliged to give up his farm, and work as a labourer.

I was born in 1791, and, being one of seven children, found myself compelled at a very early age to seek my own livelihood as best I could, so that I had not much opportunity for education, though I cannot say that I thought that much hardship at the time, being fonder of an open-air life. I was employed for some time in frightening the birds off the corn, for which I received the sum of twopence a day; after which I was advanced to sixpence a day as ploughboy, in which situation I remained until I was fourteen years of age. My father then obtained twenty pounds from a friend, with which he apprenticed me to Henry Bush, a builder living at Studland, a village in the same county, for seven years, the agreement being that my master was to find me in food, lodging, and clothes, and I was to receive no wages.

I had not been with him very long before I found that he did not suit me as a master at all well. Things went on pretty smoothly for the first month or so, that is, while the money for my apprenticeship lasted; but after that he became rather difficult to please, and besides took to allowancing me in food, which was a much more serious matter both to my mind and palate.

However, I rubbed on for about nine months, until one Sunday, when I had gone out to church in the morning and had happened to stay in the village all day, on my return home at last after dark I found the house locked up. I accordingly proceeded to Swanage, the nearest town, and called on my master's sister, who lived there, who took me in and was giving me some supper, when my master chanced to come in himself, and was very angry with me and told me to come along with him, declaring that he would pay me out in the morning. When we got home he ordered me to see if the garden gate was closed, which I thought rather strange, as it was a thing I had never had to do before; but meanwhile he slipped upstairs with a horsewhip, which he produced suddenly in the morning, and gave me a good thrashing before I had well got my clothes on. I bundled downstairs pretty much as I was, and out of the house as quick as I could, saying to myself, "This is the last thrashing I will ever receive at your hands;" and sure enough it was, for that same week I planned with another apprentice near the same place, who was under very similar circumstances to myself, to take our departure on the following Sunday; so that was the end of my apprenticeship.

And I should like here to warn any master whose eye may fall on this story not to treat any lad who is put under his care too harshly, as it is very often the means of discouraging him in the occupation he is intended to follow, and of driving him from his home, and even from his country, and to his ruin. Thus even in my case it will be seen that it was all my master's want of kindness that forced me into a very different sort of life to that which my parents intended for me; into one which, though it was not altogether so ruinous, was perhaps more perilous than many others, and on which I can only now look back in wonder that I have been spared to tell my story at all. But I must go back to the day on which myself and my companion had resolved to leave our homes, which as I have before stated was a Sunday, no better opportunity appearing by which we might get a few hours' start unbeknown to our employers. We met early in the morning, but finding that neither of us had either money or food, and I likewise wanting to get hold of my indentures, we waited until the family had left the house as usual to go to Swanage to chapel, when I made my entry into the house by the back door, which was only fastened by a piece of rope-yarn. I could not find my indentures, but in the search for them I came upon a seven-shilling piece, which I put into my pocket, as I thought it might be useful. I also cut about three or four pounds off a flitch of bacon that hung in the chimney corner, nicely marked to prevent any being lost on account of my late allowanced state. I did not study that much at the time, however, but took what I thought we should require, and when I had put it into a bag with the necessary amount of bread, we marched off together up to a place near called King's Wood, where we put a little of our bread and raw bacon out of sight, for we were both hungry. Then we went on to Wareham, a distance of about ten miles, where we changed our seven-shilling piece, and had a pint of small beer to help us in again lightening our bundle; and, after about an hour's rest, proceeded on for Poole, about nine miles from Wareham. We felt very tired, but still walked on, and gained our destination at a very late hour, owing to which we had some trouble in obtaining a lodging for the remaining part of the night, but at last we found one in a public house, where we finished our bread and bacon, together with some more beer, the best day's allowance we had had for some time past.

We slept very soundly, and in the morning went round to inquire for service on board the Newfoundland packets. We soon found a merchant of the name of Slade, who engaged us for two summers and a winter, myself for 20/. and my companion for 18/. for the whole time, and our food and lodging till the ship left the harbour. But we were not long in finding that our destination was not to be Newfoundland, for on the very next day my companion's master came to Poole in search of us, and meeting his own boy wandering about the market, soon wished to know what business he had there, and took him into custody. He likewise asked him if he had seen anything of me, and the boy told him I was in Poole, but he did not know where. I at the time was at work on board the ship, but in the evening, having fallen in with the mate, he asked me where I was going. When I said to my lodgings, beginning rather to shake, for I thought by his manner that there was something up, he told me that I had better come with him. I did so, and presently found myself with my companion's master, who finished up for the night by having me put into gaol.

Next day we were both taken on board the Swanage market-boat to go back, but when we had got as far as South Deep, near Brownsea Castle, we had to anchor, as the wind was contrary. A number of stone-boats were lying there at the time, and one of the boatmen, named Reuben Masters, took charge of me to convey me back to my master's house, as he was going by it; so we landed, and proceeded towards home. When we were about half a mile off it, however, we met my mistress, who, after inquiring where I had been, told me that her husband would have nothing more to do with me, but would send me to prison. I could have told her I did not want to trouble him any more, but I thought I would leave that for them to find out; so I went on with the man to the next gate, when, seeing an opportunity to bolt, I took it and popped over to the other side; and all I heard the man say was, "Well, you may go, and your master may run after you for himself if he likes;" so I knew there was not much to fear from him.

I ran down into the common, to a place called Agglestone, which I knew had once been a great place for foxes, and there I crawled into a hole and remained till dusk. Then I came out of my den, and again made my way to Wareham. I called this time at the Horse and Groom where, having related my story to the landlady, she kindly gave me food and lodging for the night, advising me to go back to my parents and state my master's behaviour. So next morning, after she had provided me with breakfast, and some bread and cheese to eat on the way, I set off for Dorchester.

On the road I met with two boys who were going to Poole to try and get a ship bound for Newfoundland. I wanted some companions on my journey, so I told them not to go to Poole, as the press-gang was about, and, when I had been there myself a few days before, had fired a blunderbuss at me, but I happened to pop round the corner and so had escaped. The boys did not seem fit for soldiers, or sailors either, for they looked as if they had lain in the sun for some time, and one of them was warped. When they heard my story, they turned back and kept with me. They soon began to complain of hunger, but when I asked them if they had got any money, they said they had only one shilling and a farthing, with a hundred miles to travel before they reached their home again; so I took out my bread and cheese and divided it amongst us. We were very tired and hungry when we arrived at Dorchester, and I tried to persuade them to change the shilling, but they would not. However, they gave me the farthing; it was not much certainly for a hungry boy, but it served to purchase a cake for me to devour; and then I and my companions parted, and what became of them afterwards I do not know.

CHAPTER 2

I Join the Fortieth Regiment

Dorchester was only about eight miles from my parents' house, but I had never really had one serious thought of going to them. I seemed to myself to be completely friendless, and wandered through and through the town, watching the preparations for the fair, which was to take place the next day, not being able to make up my mind what to do or where to go.

At length, more by instinct than aim, I wandered into the stable-yard of one of the principal inns, where I was brought nearer to my senses by hearing the ostler sing out sharply, "Hullo, my man, what is your business?" I told him I was a friendless boy in search of some employment by which I might get a livelihood, as I was very hungry and had no money, or something to that effect; to which he replied that if I would brush about a bit, and help him rub over the horses, he would find me plenty to eat. I soon went to work, and finished the task he gave me; and sure enough he fulfilled his share of the bargain by bringing the requisite article in the shape of a lump of bread and beef enough for two or three meals. After eating as much as I wanted, as I felt very tired, I made up a bed for myself with some straw, and putting the remainder of my meal into my handkerchief to serve as a pillow, laid myself down, and the ostler having given me a rug to pull over me, I slept soundly there the whole night.

In the morning, after I had done a little more in the stable, I walked out with my new friend into the street, where seeing some soldiers, I told him I should like to become one. He said he knew where he could enlist me, and took me straight to the rendezvous, which was in a public house, where we met a sergeant of artillery, who gave him two guineas for bringing me and myself five for coming, and when my measurement had been taken, a proceeding which was accompanied with no small amount of joking, I was put into an old soldier's coat, and with three or four yards of ribbon hanging from my cap, paraded the town with other recruits, entering and treating some one or other in almost every public-house.

It almost seemed, however, as if my hopes were again to be blighted, for in the very first house I entered, there sat a farmer from my home who knew me very well, and exclaimed on seeing me, "Hullo, young fellow, as you make your bed so you must lie on it." I entreated him not to tell my father and mother where and how he had seen me, and made my exit as quickly as possible; but later in the day I encountered another man, my father's next-door neighbour, who also recognized me immediately. I offered him the price of a gallon of ale not to say anything, and he promised, taking the money, but as soon as he got home he went to my father and acquainted him with what I was up to.

How I was spending the rest of the night meanwhile can better be conceived than described; but next morning, as I was going up to the Town Hall with an officer to be sworn in, who should meet us but my father and mother. On their telling the officer that I was an apprentice, he gave me up to them without any further trouble, except that he asked me what had become of my bounty money, and on finding that I had only seventeen shillings and sixpence left out of my whole five guineas, kindly took the care of even that off my hands. Then we marched off home, and my father went to find out what was to be done in the matter from a magistrate, who advised him to take me back to Dorchester to be tried at the next sittings; which advice being acted on, I was severely reprimanded by the bench, and given my choice of serving my time or else going to prison. Of course I chose the former, and they gave me a letter to take with me to my master. When I got downstairs I met the officer who had enlisted me, who told me that if my master was unwilling to take me back, he would enlist me again; and finding on asking me if I had any money that he had taken all I possessed, he gave me a shilling and wished me well.

My father sent me off at once with strict orders to get back to Studland as quickly as I could, and that was all I received from him either in the way of blessing or anything: so with a heavy heart I set out on my retreat from Dorchester. I had not gone very far when I was overtaken by a dairyman's cart, in which the owner gave me a lift, asking me where I was bound for. I told him a little of my story, and showed him the letter, that he might open it, and see what was inside: which, when he had done, he said I could go back quite safely, for my master would not be able to hurt me. That put me into rather better spirits, though I did not intend to go back all the same.

I rode along with the man as far as he went, and then continued on foot to a village called Winfrith, where I went into a public-house, and feeling hungry, ordered some bread and cheese. A soldier happened to be in there, who was on furlough, bound for Bridport, and the very sight of him again revived my old spirit and made me long to be like him. I got into conversation with him, and said how much I wished to be a soldier, to which he straightway answered that he could enlist me for the Fortieth Regiment Foot, which gave sixteen guineas bounty. I thought that was a great deal, and that if I got it I should not want for money for some time, so I quickly accepted his proposal: I soon found out, though, that I was very mistaken in my views about the money lasting.

I was rather afraid of finding myself in Dorchester again, so tried to persuade him to go round another way, but we at last slipped through at night, and got to Winterborne, where we put up, going on next morning in the coach to Bridport I was again baffled for a time on arriving there, for the coachman knew all about me, and remarked in a way that was no doubt meant well, that it was but yesterday that my father had got me out of the artillery. The soldier then asked me if I was an apprentice, and I thought there seemed nothing to do but to tell him I was one on which he promptly made me get down, and taking me across some fields to his home, kept me there quietly for three days.

It seemed best after that to go on to Taunton in Somerset-shire, where we went to the barracks and saw the colonel, who on the soldier telling him that he had brought me up as a recruit, asked me of what trade I was. I replied that I was a labourer, which he said was all right, for labourers made the best soldiers: but he could only give me two and a half guineas bounty: at which point we parted from him, and went to try the recruiting sergeant of the Marines, who promised us sixteen guineas bounty when I arrived at the Plymouth headquarters. This did not suit my conductor, however, as there was nothing for him after paying my coach expenses, so he asked me what I intended to do, and for his part advised me to go back to my master, saying he would not mind the expenses he had gone to for me. But as I had by this time destroyed the letter, I preferred going back to the Fortieth Regiment, so we went and again saw the colonel, who gave my companion two guineas, and sent me into barracks.

Next day I received my clothes, and in about a week more was sworn in before a magistrate, receiving my bounty at the same time. Very shortly afterwards orders came for the regiment to march to Winchester, where we remained for about a month without anything of any note occurring. I began to drill twice a day directly I joined, and soon learnt the foot drill, after which I was put on to musketry drill.

From Winchester we removed to Portsmouth, where we lay for a week, and were then ordered to Bexhill barracks in Sussex, where our First battalion was lying, and on our arrival a number of men were drafted out of our battalion, which was the Second, into the First, to make it a thousand strong, myself being one of the number. Then orders came for us to proceed to Portsmouth to embark on foreign service, our country being at the time at war with France and Spain.

CHAPTER 3

South America:
the River Plate Expedition

We passed the night before our embarkation in the town: a night to many perhaps the bitterest they had ever experienced, but to myself, on the the other hand, one mainly of joy, for I felt that I had at last outwitted my pursuers. But though I cannot say that I was yet at all repentant, it must not be thought that I felt altogether comfortable on leaving my country with all my friends and relations in it, so young as I was at the time: more especially when I considered the errand we were on, and thought that I might never return to see them again, knowing that they had not the slightest idea of where I was. I naturally felt rather timid, as all young recruits must feel on entering so soon on foreign service as I then found myself obliged to do.

But the worst and most disheartening spectacle of all was in the morning when the bugle sounded for the assembly of the regiment, for only about six women to a company of a hundred men being allowed to go with us, many who were married had to leave wives and children behind, with the thought that it might never be their lot to see them again. When the order was given to embark, the scene was quite heartrending: I could not see a dry eye in Portsmouth, and if the tears could have been collected, they might have stocked a hospital in eye-water for some months. Husband and wife, father, and child, young man and sweetheart, all had to part, and perhaps none were more affected than the last, though with least cause: it indeed was dreadful to view.

I myself was much affected, but it was at the woes of others, for I had not one to throw so much as a parting glance at myself; and thus, amid the cheers of the crowd, and with the band playing the tune of *The Girl I left behind me*, we embarked.

Then I felt quite freed from my pursuers, but in getting out of the frying-pan I soon found myself into the fire, for as it afterwards proved I had many men to deal with more difficult than even my old master had been. Thus it is that many are apt to dislike and leave their employment through trifles, and in the search for a better often only get a worse one, much to their disappointment.

The next day we drew out of Portsmouth harbour on our route to South America, and sea-sickness soon commencing on board, I was, the worse luck for myself, one of the number that succumbed to it This lasted for nearly a week, during the whole of which time we scarcely ate anything; but when we got better, I think our appetites were such that we could have readily finished a donkey with a hamper of greens.

We had good weather until we reached the tropics, when a dead calm followed for a fortnight. As we were nearly upon the Equinoctial line, the usual ceremony of shaving took place, which was no doubt very amusing to those who escaped by treating the sailors to a bottle of rum, or those who had crossed the Line before; but to us on whom the barber, who was the sailor who had crossed the Line most often, operated, it was not so pleasant For the satisfaction of some who may not quite understand the method of that interesting custom, I will give the routine, at least as it happened on board our ship, though I cannot altogether say whether the same is pursued universally. A large tub of water was placed on deck, and each one who was to be performed on, sat in turn on the edge; then the barber stepped forward and lathered his face all over with tar and grease, and with a piece of iron hoop as a razor scraped it off again; after which he pushed him backwards into the tub, leaving him to crawl out anyhow and sneak off to clean himself. All passed off very well, however, as there was plenty of rum provided to drink from those officers and men who were more disposed to join in the pay than the play.

During the calms, we amused ourselves fishing for dolphins, and practising for the first time with ball-cartridge, a bottle being corked and flung overboard as far as possible to serve as a target, and a dollar being offered to the first man who could break it, each one firing once. No one broke it, but I got a glass of grog from the major for being the nearest; so near that I made the bottle spin round. The major remarked that if I went so close as that to a Spaniard I should make him shake; and he likewise asked me what trade I was in before I joined the army. As I knew I was too far from England now to be sent back, I told him that I was a builder's apprentice; and he only said, "Well done, my boy, so you prefer knocking down houses in the enemy's country to putting them up in your own? "Certainly at this moment we were having an easy place, but there was many a time afterwards when I should like to have been given the choice of laying bricks again.

After spending about a fortnight in this way, a fair wind blew up, and we proceeded on our voyage. We called in at Rio Janeiro, the capital of the Brazilian Empire, lying upon the western side of the entrance to a fine bay which forms the harbour. Our chief object for putting in there was to take in water and provisions; and whilst we were anchored there we went on shore, and the Queen of Portugal reviewed us. Next day she sent a quantity of onions and pumpkins on board as a present, which we found very acceptable. We stayed there about a fortnight, sailing on next further south to Maldonado, the rendezvous of the fleet, whence after being joined by five thousand troops under Sir Samuel Auchmuty, the whole fleet moved on to Monte Video and anchored.

We lost no time on our arrival there, but early the next morning boats were ordered alongside the troopships to convey us on shore, which movement, as the enemy was on the banks about fifteen thousand strong to receive us, put rather a nasty taste into our mouths, there seeming nothing but death or glory before us. The signal was hoisted from the admiral's ship, and we started for the shore amid the fire of the enemy's artillery. They killed and wounded a few of our men, and sank some of the boats, but as soon as we struck the shore, we jumped out, and forming line in the water, fired a volley and charged, soon driving them from their position on the bank. We found even as early as then that Spaniards were not very difficult to encounter. In case of a retreat, our boats were still within our reach, but having gained the victory, we had no need of them, stopping where we were on the banks all night.

Some field-pieces were next sent on shore, and likewise a number of sailors with drag-ropes to work them, as we had no horses with us, and up to this time no artillery. The country was rather favourable for the sailors, being very level and mostly green pasture, so that they kept along pretty easily, seeming just in their glory, all this being new work to them. After some little firing from the cannon the enemy retreated into the town, which was well fortified. We placed an outlying picket of some three hundred men to watch the enemy's manoeuvres, while the body of our army encamped in the rear in a line stretching from sea to sea, so that the town standing upon a projecting piece of land, all communication from the mainland was cut off. The country around meanwhile abounded with ducks, geese, turkeys, fowls, and plenty of sheep and bullocks, which it may be made sure our men found oftentimes very providential.

On the third day of our encampment the Spaniards sallied out of the town to surprise our picket, which being overpowered was obliged to retreat, leaving two grenadiers wounded on the field, whom the Spaniards much to our horror deliberately cut into pieces. But on the body of our army coming up and charging them, a terrible slaughter ensued on their retreat to the town, which amply repaid us for our two grenadiers; as far as I am able to state, there could not have been less than three thousand killed and wounded, for the next day we had actually to bury two thousand of them. Our loss was a mere nothing.

I remember that I happened to be placed that night on sentry at the road leading to the town, and not far from a hole where we had buried five or six hundred of the enemy. It was the most uncomfortable two hours' sentry I had ever spent as yet, and I kept my eyes more on the place where the dead were than on the road I was placed to watch, not having altogether forgotten the absurd ghost stories of my own country. I in a way began to think, too, that I had done a good many things I should have liked not to, and to regret for the first time leaving my apprenticeship, my father, mother, and friends, to follow a life so dangerous as I now found this to be, with nothing to expect, as I thought, but to be myself numbered with the slain. I soon became more hardened, however, as I was more and more mixed up in similar or worse affairs than these slight brushes with a weak enemy had proved to be. However, at this juncture I took the opportunity to send my first letter home, so as to satisfy the folks there of my whereabouts, though I kept from them the more perilous part of my story.

We reported to the general the circumstances of the Spaniards' barbarity to our wounded comrades, and the answer he gave was that we were to repay them in their own coin. I may mention here that we all thought Sir Samuel a most excellent commander. He always delighted most in a good rough-looking soldier with a long beard and greasy haversack, who he thought was the sort of man most fit to meet the enemy. It was chiefly owing to his dislike to dandyism that wearing long hair with powder, which was the fashion then for the smart soldier, was done away with soon after we landed in the enemy's country; of course also partly because it was so difficult to get the powder.

We never found the Spaniards sally out of the town after this to engage us, as I expect they did not much like the warm reception they had received. We set to work building up batteries and breastworks, some three hundred of us being sent to cut down a copse of peach-trees that was near to make gabions and fascines to form them with. When our fortifications were completed, which was in a very few days, we began bombarding the town, for which purpose we had brought up our twenty-four pounders from the men-of-war. After about four days' play we made a breach by knocking down the gate and part of the wall, which was six feet thick, and though the enemy, repaired it at night with a quantity of bullocks' hides filled with earth, next morning as early as two o'clock we advanced to storm the town.

Captain Renny of ours commanded the forlorn hope. The ladders were placed against the hides of earth, and we scaled them under a heavy fire from the Spaniards. We found the earth better stuff to encounter than stone, and though our poor captain fell in the breach whilst nobly leading on his men, we succeeded in forcing our way into the town, which was soon filled with the reinforcements that followed us. We drove the enemy from the batteries, and massacred with sword and bayonet all whom we found carrying arms: the general's orders being not to plunder or enter any house, or injure any woman, child, or man not carrying arms, or fire a shot until daylight On our approach to the gunwharf of the town, we found some twenty or thirty negroes chained to the guns, whom we spared and afterwards found very useful, chiefly in burying the dead.

When the heat of the fighting was subsided, the drums beat to assembly in the square, and orders were then given for the massacre to be stayed, but that all the prisoners were to be taken that we could lay our hands on. Our troops were accordingly despatched to the forts and batteries, and nearly three thousand prisoners were taken; the governor of the town giving himself up with all the forts except the citadel, where there was a separate general in command. The governor said he had nothing to do with this, so Sir Samuel sent a flag of truce to know if the commander would give the place up. The answer being "No," three or four riflemen were placed on a tower sufficiently high and near to the citadel for the purpose of, if possible, picking out the general and shooting him. This was soon effected, for on his appearing for a walk on the ramparts in his full uniform, one of the men shot him dead: and when the Spaniards found that they had lost their commander, they soon became disheartened, and lowering the drawbridge, came out of the citadel and gave themselves up. Part of our troops immediately took possession, pulling down the Spanish colours and hoisting the English flag from the town and citadel in their stead. We took about four thousand prisoners in all, who were sent on board ship; but where they were taken to afterwards I am not able to state.

CHAPTER 4

Colonia

Now that we had got possession of a fine town, we could lie up comfortably, only having to put out three or four hundred men on picket round the walls and see that the gates of the town were closed every night at sunset and not opened till daylight in the morning, and then feeling that we could make ourselves quite at home. The inhabitants were meanwhile not altogether deprived of their livelihood, as our general issued a proclamation that they should open their shops and carry on their business as usual: and if any declined to open, he was kind enough to send parties to do it for them.

During the time that we lay there, which I should think was at least five months, the only things that occurred that could be called out of the way were, I am sorry to say, of rather an unpleasant nature. One thing was that a sergeant and corporal of the Spanish army came in disguise and tried to enlist any of our men who would join their service; and unfortunately a sergeant named Goodfellow, one of my own regiment, accepted their proposals, tempted by the heavy bounty they offerred. But while passing out of the town in disguise with the Spaniards, he was met and recognized by the general himself and his staff: a most unlucky encounter for the three runaways, for they were brought back again and put under charge immediately, and a court-martial ordered on them next day. Our colonel, however, implored so hard for our sergeant's life on account of the regiment's late good conduct in the field, that the general granted it, and changed his sentence to one of transportation for life: but the Spaniards were not quite so leniently dealt with, for they were tried and hanged, to make sure that they could not repeat their mischievous practices.

We also found among the prisoners an Irishman who had somehow got away from us over on to the wrong side, and had been fighting against us. He was tried and sentenced to be hanged, and we all had to march up next day to witness his execution and take example from it. But his life was not destined to end here, for the rope was not altogether a strong one, and he was fortunate enough when he fell to break it Directly his feet touched ground he begged hard for mercy, and the rope had made such a terrible mark on his neck that I suppose the general thought he had been hanged enough: so he was sent into hospital, and when he recovered, transported for the rest of the life that had thus been given back to him. While he was on his way down the town to go on board the vessel, I should think that if he had one dollar given him, he had at least half a peck, though I do not expect they would be much use to him where he was going to. I never heard any more of him, but I don't suppose many men could say that they had been hanged and then transported afterwards.

Another case of desertion was that of an officer's servant, who went away with the greater part of his master's clothes, taking with him likewise a Spanish lady; he was lucky enough to get off safe, and nothing was heard of him afterwards. This was not at all a rare temptation, though, that was put in our soldiers' way; for I was myself offered a fortune by a Spanish gentleman, together with his daughter, if I would desert and remain in the country. Whenever he met me about he would treat me to anything I liked to name, which I sometimes found very acceptable, and he would often give me money as well, in hopes of gaining me over in time. He had more chances of making up to me, for I forgot to mention that I had received a slight wound in the left leg in storming the town, which kept me limping about and partially disabled from duty for nearly a fortnight; but I don't think he would have minded his daughter not marrying me in particular, so long as he could persuade some one. But he happened one day to leave his horse tied up close to our main guard while he went into a kind of public-house, and occupied himself treating some of our men; and the fact being discovered by those outside that his stirrups were of solid gold, when he came out again one of them was missing. It must have weighed at least a pound, so naturally he thought it worth while reporting the circumstance to the colonel, and a search was made; but no clue could be found to the missing stirrup, so he had to ride away as best he could with only the other one; so he only came off a loser in the end, and he never got his daughter married after all.

After staying in the town for the time stated, a thousand of us were despatched up the river Rio de la Plata to a small place called Colonia, where an army of Spaniards about four or five thousand strong was lying. We landed with ease, and the enemy retreated out of the place after firing a few shots, leaving it in our hands, so that we again found ourselves for a time in comfortable quarters. We placed pickets of two or three hundred men round the place, and fixed a *chevaux de frise* in the gate, formed of very sharp and pointed swords stuck very thickly into a beam which was made to turn on its axis: rather an awkward instrument to face if one is not used to it Duty at this place was rather hard, owing to there being so few of us, and such a number on picket or at work building some batteries for our better protection.

At the picket-house, which was some distance from the town, there lived a soap-boiler and tallow-chandler, who was very kind to us while we were there on duty, killing a bullock almost every night for our use, as he only required the skin and tallow, and any one may suppose that two hundred hungry men knew what to do with the rest of it. An incident took place during our stay at his house which will show how well disposed he was towards us. We had passed a very quiet week there, when one night the Spaniards passed our picket secretly in the darkness, fired a volley into the town, and then immediately retreated. Our picket only just managed to get through safely into the town, leaving one of our men asleep in the picket-house, and he must certainly have met his death if he had been caught there singly; but the tallow-chandler, though himself a Spaniard, concealed him under a quantity of dry hides while the enemy were scouring the place in search of stragglers, and so saved his life. In consequence of this surprise, still heavier duty was afterwards put upon us, the picket having to be augmented to prevent further annoyance.

Two or three days after this had occurred the tallow-chandler was sent for to join the Spanish army, no doubt because their general suspected him of favouring the English; but he would not go until he had obtained our colonel's advice, which was that he should go by all means, and if he could conveniently come back with full particulars of the enemy's strength he should be rewarded. As far as I can remember, he had been away about ten days, when he again made his appearance with the requisite information. What reward he got I cannot say, but as the result of his tidings, about two or three days afterwards we were called under arms at midnight and supplied with half a pound of beef for each man; the order then being given to return to our lodgings for two hours, and at the end of that time to fall in again. Meanwhile a number of sailors came from on board our ships to take charge of the town during our absence, we being now bound for some place as yet unknown to us.

A little after two in the morning we left the town with an Indian for our guide. We asked in the best manner that we could where we were going to, but all we could understand from him was that we were on the way to fight some Spaniards, which of course we had pretty well guessed before, and that we should have some four or five thousand of them to encounter. This last bit of news made us think that we were going to have hard nuts to crack, but we found them a very cowardly sort of folk to deal with, for after marching some five or six miles, we despatched skirmishing parties, who fell in with their picket and took a few prisoners, and soon made the others retreat without doing anything further than to send up some rockets to alarm the body of the enemy.

We marched on still further till we came nearly up to them, when we found a river in our way, fortunately it was not very deep, so we waded through it under a fire from the Spanish cannon, which killed two of our men while in the act of crossing; and as soon as we were over we formed line and advanced towards the enemy, who lay on some fine rising ground in our front They had some few pieces of cannon with them, and opened the first fire with both cannon and musketry, but every shot seemed to rise over our heads, and I don't think that volley killed a man. We were up and at them like dragons, wounding and taking their general with about a hundred and fifty other prisoners; likewise a stand of colours, three pieces of cannon, and their baggage. Moreover, we found a nice breakfast cooking for us in the shape of fowls, geese, turkeys, beef, rice, and *calavancos,* though the latter were rather too warm with cayenne pepper and garlic, all of which the enemy had had to leave in his hurry, and which came in very acceptably at the end of a long march.

The colonel ordered everything to be taken from the prisoners we had made, as that was how he had been served himself when he had been taken prisoner at Buenos Ayres, so we set to clearing them of all they possessed, their money, which amounted to about two thousand dollars, their clothes, and even their boots. I had a very narrow escape while the plunder was going on. I entered one of the enemy's storehouses, at one end of which a quantity of bullocks' hides were lying, at a sufficient distance from the wall to allow a man to pass or hide behind them; and there beside the heap stood a Spaniard whom I knew well, as he had sold cakes to us while we were at Colonia, and who now offered me a pot of honey to eat. I had my misgivings, however, so made motion for him to eat first, for fear of poison; and at the same time, casting my eye to the left, I saw a Spaniard emerge from between the hides and the wall with a pistol, which he levelled at me. I became pretty active, as may be supposed under the circumstances, and managed to guard it off; but the shot whizzed very close to my head nevertheless, which made me very much enraged with the man, and determined he should not escape. Unfortunately for him, one of our dismounted cavalry, an Irishman, came in, and on my telling him there was a Spaniard behind the hides, who had just fired a pistol at me, "Tare an' 'ounds," says he, "I'll fetch him out; you stand at one end to stop him with your bayonet while I drive him out" So Paddy went round with his sword, and after a little exercise behind, "Look out comrade," he sang out, "he's coming;" and sure enough I skewered him to the wall by driving my bayonet right through his body, while Paddy came out and finished him by splitting his head, nearly in two with his heavy sword, remarking as he did it, "Bad luck to ye, I don't think ye'll ever shoot another Englishman, or Irishman either." The other man had meanwhile made off.

We had taken amongst other things about twenty barrels of gunpowder and a quantity of cigars, which latter, owing to the carelessness of one man, proved to be more plague than profit; for whilst most of us were smoking, one of the company, going near the powder, happened to let a spark fall from his cigar, which resulted in twelve men being blown into the air: and though none were killed on the spot, they were so frightfully burnt that several died on reaching Colonia. I believe all that we lost actually killed by the enemy's hand were the two men who fell in crossing the river. We gave ten dollars to each of the widows of the men killed, and the rest of the prize-money was divided.

CHAPTER 5

Buenos Ayres

As we had effected all that was wanted at San Pedro, which was the name of the place where we had been carrying on these operations, we returned to Colonia, dragging back the guns laden with our wounded, and taking with us the prisoners, who had to walk along barefooted, as we had availed ourselves of their boots. On our arrival at Colonia our sailors saluted us when they saw the number of our prisoners and the three pieces of cannon we had taken, giving "three cheers for the brave soldiers." The prisoners were then sent on board a ship that was lying in the river, and an outlying picket having been posted as usual, the rest of us remained comfortably in the town. Next day the colonel gave orders for everything belonging to the prisoners, such as clothes, &c, to be brought out, offering a fair price for them to be returned to their proper owners, which showed of what a good disposition he really was: only he had allowed us to take the things before as an example.

We remained here about a month this time, when General Whitelock came out with a reinforcement and took the command from Sir Samuel Auchmuty, and soon afterwards, some troops being left in charge of Monte Video, the rest proceeded to Buenos Ayres, calling at Colonia on the way to pick up our little squad. We landed some miles before coming to Buenos Ayres, intending, if possible, to storm the back of the town, as it was strongly fortified on the side towards the coast. We were thus obliged to march inland and form encampments, the first of which was situated a little way from where we landed.

An incident took place here, which was attended by the death of two men, a corporal and a private, and likewise the very narrow escape of a second private. They were engaged in plundering one of the Indian huts, when the inhabitants fell on them armed, and, catching the corporal round the neck with a lasso, soon dragged him away, at the same time knocking the private down and stabbing him; the other private only escaped back to the regiment after receiving a sabre-wound which carried the skin and hair off the back of his head. This was a great glory to the natives; they stuck the corporal's head on a pole and carried it in front of their little band when on the march. They also made use of the rifle and ammunition they had taken from him to fire at times into our camp, but fortunately it was a very harmless sort of practice.

Next day we again resumed our march, encamping again at night. I remember that night was very foggy, and an officer and some men having gone out in search of bullocks for the supply of the army, the officer was very nearly lassoed by an Indian who came on him suddenly in the darkness. Fortunately he had the presence of mind to ride after him, which saved his life, for so the Indian could not pull him over; and then he managed to cut the lasso with his sword.

As we marched along on our next day's journey, about two hundred Indians kept following us, the foremost of them wearing our dead corporal's jacket, and carrying his head—I do not exactly know for what reason, but perhaps they thought a good deal more of a dead man's head than we should feel disposed to do. We went on for some distance through a great many orange-gardens, till we came to a lane thickly hedged in on both sides, which was entered by a gate, and there, after the body of our army had passed through, some few men, including myself, waited in ambush for the Indians, having a reserve placed a short distance down the lane in case of a combat. The Indians soon approached, but seemed to have some misgivings, though we could not exactly understand what they said. There being only a few of us, not quite twenty in all, I rather shook in my shoes on seeing their number; but we soon found there was very little occasion for this, for on our firing directly the front party had passed the gate, killing two of them and wounding and capturing their chief, who was the one who was so proud of his head, the rest fled for their lives, not liking the smell and much less the taste of our gunpowder. We picked up the wounded man and carried him, and left him, more dead than alive, in a neighbouring village.

On nearing Buenos Ayres the Light Brigade was ordered on in front, under the command of Colonel Pack, who soon succeeded in taking the Bull Ring battery, for Buenos Ayres was much more easy to take than Monte Video, as it was very slightly fortified towards the country. There were some cannons placed at the end of each street, but they proved a very small difficulty to be overcome, as there seemed nobody efficient to work them and after passing these, our soldiers were soon in possession of the city. Then they hoisted the King's flag on a convent and waited, expecting every minute that the body of our army would come up; but instead of this, General Whitelock encamped about a mile out of the town and remained there. If he had attended properly to his business he would have followed up and relieved the brigade, but as it was, the Spaniards rallied and overpowered it. I was with the main body, and so was not able to enter the city to see what was going on. We all fell under arms when we heard the muskets at work, waiting for the general's orders to advance: but there we lay the whole night, not doing a stroke, and next day we re-embarked for Monte Video, having come to some terms, though we were ignorant of that at the time. We remained at Monte Video some two months longer, during which interval the ships taken in the harbour were offered for sale, but the inhabitants refusing to buy them, we loaded some ourselves with hides, tallow, and cocoa, and the rest, which were not worth bringing home, were towed out to the mouth of the harbour and set on fire. The Spaniards had previously blown up a very fine frigate to prevent it falling into our hands. Part of our army was then embarked for the East Indies and the Cape of Good Hope, whilst we others went on an expedition about a hundred miles up the Rio de la Plata to get fresh water, and when we returned proceeded on our way homewards from that part of the world.

The first part of our voyage was very pleasant, the troops in general, keeping very healthy; but when we had sailed some distance, we had a dead calm for a considerable time, which made us much longer on our voyage than we had thought for, and consequently our water supply ran very short, and had to be served out in allowances of half a pint a day. A small supply, however, fortunately came before long. Our captain, seeing a cloud in the distance, foretold that we were going to have a thunderstorm, and ordered the scupper-holes to be stopped, and all except the watch to remain below. I happened to be one of the watch at the time, and well I remember how it very shortly after began to thunder and lighten, the rain falling in torrents for two or three hours; it was the heaviest thunderstorm I had ever witnessed. We baled up some twenty or more casks of water, which was none the better, perhaps, for there being pigs, fowls, geese, and turkeys all over the deck, but still was very acceptable to us in our parched state, as till that we had had to cook our food and wash ourselves in salt water only.

During the storm our mainmast was struck by the lightning, which split a piece off it from top to bottom, but fortunately did not disable it; but a sad mishap befell one of our men while sitting at mess at the time, for he was struck dead, his shirt being burnt in places like tinder, and his mess-tin being likewise turned black, while the top of a bayonet that was standing close to the unfortunate man was melted like lead. The blow had shaken our little bark so terribly that the captain ordered the pumps to be tried; fortunately there was no leakage to be found, but the lightning must have got well down below, for on opening the main hatchway the sulphur came up enough to suffocate any one.

After the storm, the calm still continued, and we had to amuse ourselves as best we could with fishing; a few days after a breeze sprang up, but it was foul for England, and we had to knock about till a more favourable one blew up, which finally landed us in the Cove of Cork. We spent the Christmas of 1807 on board, sending on shore for raisins, flour, fat, and beer, and so being enabled to enjoy ourselves very comfortably.

CHAPTER 6

The Peninsula:
the Battle of Vimeira

We had already laid in our sea stock in preparation to start for England, when we found ourselves disappointed of our hopes, for orders came for us to land in Ireland; and we had to march to Cork and thence to various other places for six months, nothing of any particular note happening during the while; and at the end of it, orders again came for us to embark for Portugal, to drive the French from there, and from the Spanish dominions. Thus after we had been in open war against the Spaniards, who for the time had been in alliance with the French, or rather had been forced to be so, now that Buonaparte had overrun their own country and kindled hatred against himself, these same Spaniards had made peace with us, and sent to us for assistance to drive him out of their country: so that we had to go and fight for the very nation we' had been a few months before opposing in Monte Video, Buenos Ayres, and Colonia.

After we had all embarked we had still to lie in Cork Harbour, waiting for the English fleet, and then we sailed from the Irish coast, about twelve thousand strong, under Sir Arthur Wellesley, on the 12th of July, 1808. We first touched at Corunna to make arrangements with the Spaniards, and their advice being to land in Portugal, we went to Mondego Bay, near the town of Figueras, where we landed, leaving our baggage on board. After about five days' march we were joined by General Spencer, and next day our advanced guard had a slight engagement with the enemy at Rorica. Thence we marched on to Vimeira, and were joined by Generals Anstruther and Acland with more reinforcements, and Sir Hugh Dalrymple took the head command from Sir Arthur Wellesley

The village of Vimeira stood in a valley with a fine range of hills to the westward, and a ridge of heights to the east. Our brigades were stationed on the mountains to the west, whilst our cavalry was posted in the valley, and General Anstruther's brigade lay to the east.

On the first night of our encampment there, two of my comrades and myself were strolling over the hills together, when we fell in with a hive of bees, weighing I should think at least a hundredweight, which we carried back into the camp: not without difficulty, however, for we found them very uncivil passengers to carry, and our faces and hands were fearfully stung; but our honey and grapes, for we had profited too from being encamped in some very fine vineyards, paid us for this a little. Next morning we proceeded to make our breakfast off the same materials, but we were not destined to finish very quietly, for in the midst of our meal we were disturbed by the near approach of the enemy, and were immediately ordered under arms. The right of our line was engaged at least two hours before a general engagement took place on our side, which was the left, but we were skirmishing with the enemy the whole time. I remember this well, on account of a Frenchman and myself being occupied in firing at each other for at least half an hour without doing anyone any injury; but he took a pretty straight aim at me once, and if it had not been for a tough front-rank man that I had, in the shape of a cork-tree, his shot must have proved fatal, for I happened to be straight behind the tree when the bullet embedded itself in it. I recollect saying at the time, "Well done, front-rank man, thee doesn't fall at that stroke," and unfortunately for the Frenchman, a fellow-comrade, who was left-handed, came up to me very soon afterwards, and asked me how I was getting on. I said badly, and told him there was a Frenchman in front, and we had been trying to knock each other over for some time, without either of us having been able to succeed; on which he asked me where he was, that he might have a try at him. I pointed out the thicket behind which the Frenchman was, and he prepared his rifle so as to catch him out in his peeping manoeuvres, but not without himself, as well as I, being well covered by my old front-rank man. By-and-by Mr. Frenchman again made his peep round the bush, but it was his last, for my comrade, putting his rifle to his left shoulder, killed him at the first shot

After we had been thus employed in skirmishing for some time, a large body of French made their appearance in our front Our artillery greeted them pretty sharply, ploughing furrows through them with ball and throwing them into a confused state, after which our columns advanced under General Spencer, our cannon still playing over our heads, until we got within a short distance of the enemy, when we fired and charged them, driving them from the position they had occupied after some very severe fighting well kept up for some time on both sides, and capturing about seven pieces of cannon, with ammunition waggons. The loss of the French at this place could not have been much less than two thousand, though some have reported it less and some more; but it is very hard to arrive at a just calculation. Our loss was reported to have been about seven hundred.

After the battle was ended we marched on towards Lisbon, passing on our way about a hundred and fifty carts laden with the enemy's wounded. When we arrived at Lisbon we encamped, so that the French had no means of communication with the city; as, our fleet lying in or near the mouth of the harbour, and our army stopping all approach from the land, the French in the city were blocked in. On the first night of our encampment the inhabitants illuminated the part where we lay. We were not destined, however, to be outside the city long, for on the leaders of our army and the French coming to some terms, the French left with the honours of war, and gladly embarked from the harbour in September. These were the very troops with whom at a later period we had to contend.

When the enemy had left Lisbon we took up our quarters in the city, amid the joy and enthusiasm of the inhabitants, who shouted in triumph as the French left, and held illuminations even on the vessels in the harbour for several successive nights afterwards.

Lisbon then on every side still exhibited marks of that terrible earthquake which almost completely destroyed it in the year 1755. It was situated on the right bank of the Tagus, near its mouth, which forms a very fine harbour; and it stood chiefly on very precipitous hills, of which the highest was occupied by the fine castle of Saint George, which was indeed the principal object that attracted the eye anywhere from the city. The great squares contained some magnificent edifices, noteworthy for the fineness of their pillars. The streets were narrow and winding and dirty, and indeed after the French had left the whole city was in a most desolate state; but the general view of the city and its environs from the harbour at a distance was very beautiful, the sides of the hills being clothed with plantations and numberless vineyards, and the buildings extending for a mile and a half or two miles along the coast

Sir Hugh Dalrymple, Sir Arthur Wellesley, and some other of the chief leaders of our army were then recalled to England to communicate the circumstances of the terms that had been arrived at in Portugal between the two armies: as the rulers, and indeed all classes in England received the first reports of them with indignation. This was the reason that the inquiry was made, of which the fruits were that Sir Arthur Wellesley was decided on as the proper person to take the head command of our troops in the Peninsula.

During our stay in Lisbon our regiment fell ill and was obliged to be returned unfit for service, which state of things lasted about two months. But as soon as Sir Arthur Wellesley returned as commander-in-chief, we were ordered into Spain, in company with five thousand Spaniards, to join Sir John Moore's army. We had a long and tedious march until we reached a place called Seville, where we encamped for several weeks, on account of Sir John Moore having been obliged to retreat; and the French cutting off our communication, we had to proceed to Cadiz and there embark again for Lisbon.

I must here relate a circumstance which took place before I proceeded from Seville, which, although not very creditable to myself, is of too great importance as an event in my life to be omitted. I absented myself without leave from guard for twenty-four hours, and when I returned I found I had jumped into a fine scrape, for I was immediately put into the guard-room, and a drumhead court-martial was ordered on me. It was the first offence to cause one to be held on me, but that did not screen me much, and I was sentenced to four hundred lashes. I felt ten times worse on hearing this sentence than I ever did on entering any battle-field; in fact, if I had been sentenced to be shot, I could not have been more in despair, for my life at that time seemed of very little consequence to me. My home and my apprenticeship days again ran in my head, but even these thoughts soon lost themselves as I neared the spot where my sentence was to be carried out. I found the regiment assembled all ready to witness my punishment: the place chosen for it was the square of a convent. As soon as I had been brought in by the guard, the court-martial was read over me by the colonel, and then I was ordered to strip, which I did firmly and without using any of the help that was offered me, as I had by that time got hardened to my lot I was then lashed to the halberds, and the colonel gave the order for the drummers to commence, each one having to give me twenty-five lashes in turn. I bore it very well until I had received a hundred and seventy-five, when I became so enraged with the pain that I pushed the halberds, which did not stand at all firm, on account of their being planted on stones, right across the square, amid the laughter of the regiment The colonel, I suppose, thinking then that I had had sufficient, ordered, in the very words, "the sulky rascal down," and perhaps a more true word could not have been spoken, as indeed I was sulky, for I did not give vent to a single sound the whole time, though the blood ran down my trousers from top to bottom. I was unbound and the corporal hove my shirt and jacket over my shoulders and conveyed me to the hospital, presenting about as miserable a picture as I possibly could.

Perhaps it was as good a thing for me as could then have occurred, as it prevented me from committing any greater crimes which might have gained me other severer punishments and at last brought me to my ruin; but for all that it was a great trial for me, and I think that a good deal of that kind of punishment might have been abandoned with great credit to those who ruled our army; for it is amazing to think of four hundred lashes being ordered on a man young as I was, and undergoing all the privations of a most sanguinary war, just for an offence, and that the first, which might have been overlooked, or at any rate treated with less punishment and a severe reprimand.

CHAPTER 7

The Battle of Talavera

I remained in hospital about three weeks, and on coming out I was transferred from the Light into the Grenadier company.

As I before said, on leaving Seville, which I did in a pretty well marked state, of which I bear the remembrances on my back to this day upwards of fifty years since, we marched to Cadiz and encamped there, intending to embark for Lisbon, Sir John Moore's army having been by that time repulsed by sheer force of numbers, and himself killed at Corunna. On that night an English wine-merchant asked permission to give each man in our regiment a pint of wine and each woman half that quantity, with a pound of bread apiece; and accordingly we were all drawn up in line, and marched into a tremendous cellar, big enough, had they been so disposed, to have admitted the whole regiment, with two doors one at each end, at one of which we entered to receive our share, and went out by the other. He likewise invited the officers to dine with him; and so that night, after drinking the merchant's little kindnes, as we most of us did to pretty quick time, we slept a good deal sounder.

Next day we embarked for Lisbon, and after landing there we proceeded some miles up the country to join Sir Arthur's army in Castello Branco, making up altogether about twenty thousand English and sixty or eighty thousand Allies.

We then advanced across a fine plain, which I should think was more famed for hares than anything else, for I never saw any place that swarmed so with that kind of game. They were running in all directions, and often even right into our lines, for they are stupid animals when frightened, as they then were by the noise our men made; and I managed to kill one with the muzzle of my musket, and sold it to the captain of my company for a dollar.

The bands played each before its own regiment as we crossed the plain, and Sir Arthur Wellesley took the opportunity of reviewing the Spanish troops as they passed. They looked a fine enough set of men, but they were fit for scarcely anything except to fall into disorder and confusion, as we had already found when we had taken the field against some of them at Monte Video, Colonia, and Buenos Ayres, the smell of powder often seeming to cause them to be missing when wanted, either from not having been properly disciplined, or else because they had not good officers to command them, this, of course, now bringing the brunt of most of the battles on us.

We often passed marks of the enemy's encampments, and even encamped at or near the same places ourselves, as close as possible to some river or large supply of water, a small quantity being of little use for the purposes of a large body of men like our army, accompanied as it was, too, by horses and wagons and such things. We never caught sight of the enemy, however, till we got to Talavera, where we came to an engagement with the French on the 27th and 28th of July, 1809. The whole of our line there extended for about two miles, and at times the whole of it was joining in the general engagement, which came more hot upon us for the reason before described; a great number of the Spaniards even throwing down their arms and fleeing, for which conduct their general, Cuesta, ordered them to be decimated; but eventually, on the entreaty of Sir Arthur Wellesley, only about forty of them were killed. General Cuesta, however, really wanted quite as much leading on as his men, as he was often very obstinate, and refused to fight when called upon by Sir Arthur Wellesley.

After the first day's battle we encamped on the ground we then occupied, but the French made another and unexpected attack on us at night, and at one time had almost gained the heights, but we repulsed them at last, though after that we had to lie on our arms, expecting every minute to be again attacked. Some little altercation occurred with the Spaniards very early in the morning, but it only lasted a short time; however, about five or six o'clock the French columns were seen in motion towards our left, and very soon afterwards they ascended the height to attack us, and were only driven back by the heavy fire of our musketry, leaving the ground strewn with their dead. At eleven or twelve o'clock in the day the firing ceased, and a period of truce was allowed for both armies to collect their wounded, and convey them to the rear, where, as they lay often intermixed, a friendly intercourse sprang up between them, the Allies and French often going so far as to shake hands with each other.

At one or two o'clock the enemy again advanced and re-commenced with a heavy cannonade and an attack on the whole British lines, but after some very brisk fighting on both sides we repulsed them for the third time, and obliged them to retreat with a loss of some thousands and a few pieces of cannon, the British loss being about a thousand killed and three or four thousand wounded. A very dreadful occurrence happened after the battle, for the long dry grass in which many of the wounded were lying caught fire, and many were scorched to death before assistance could be brought to con-vey them to hospital in Talavera. We lay that night in much the same state as on that previous, expecting to see our noble enemy again, but we were mistaken, for most of them took themselves off during the night, and in the morning only their rear-guard could be seen.

Next month commenced by Sir Arthur Wellesley leav-ing the Spanish general Cuesta in charge of Talavera and the wounded, while on the 3rd he proceeded to Oropesa, where he expected to come up with and engage Soult's army. But he had not been there long before he found the obstinate Cuesta, upon hearing that the enemy was on his flank, had abandoned Talavera, thus leaving nearly the whole of the British wound-ed unprotected. The conduct of Cuesta in thus retreating and abandoning the position and the charge entrusted to him, was almost too much for Sir Arthur to bear, particularly as it was afterwards found that there was no need for it, as the enemy was at some distance off, and not in the least interfering with the Spanish army's movements. So in this case we would have been much better without his services altogether.

From Oropesa we advanced through a country abounding with difficulties, the army suffering much during this march from the heat of the weather, the long exposure, insufficient food, and bad roads, and illness being very prevalent. Our provisions rarely exceeded two pounds of meat a day; and sometimes a pint of wheat took the place of one of the pounds of meat, with occasionally, but very rarely, a little flour. Our way of cooking the wheat was to boil it like rice, or sometimes, if convenient, we would crack the kernel between two flat stones and then boil it, making a kind of thick paste out of it. This having so little bread or other vegetable substance to eat with our meat was one of the great causes of illness.

We halted at or near Val de la Casa as our next stage for Oropesa, and two days after that at Delei-tosa; and from there we were marched to Xaracego, whence, through lack of provisions, we were obliged to proceed to Badajoz, arriving there after being about a fortnight on the road. On leaving Talavera our clothes had been completely threadbare, and now, through having no change for so long we were smothered with vermin. When we had been a little while in Badajoz, however, we were supplied with new clothes, linen, blankets, and great coats, our old ones being burnt; and more live stock was destroyed in the process than there were troops in the country at the time.

Whilst we were staying at Badajoz, numbers of us fell sick daily, and amongst them was unfortunately myself. We were conveyed to a Portuguese town some four leagues from Badajoz, called Elvas, which was the strongest fortified town in Portugal, being very little more than two leagues from the frontier of Spain. It was situated at the summit of a lofty hill, and at the other side of a valley was a still higher hill, on the top of which was built another strong fort, the two together being called Elvas. We invalids occupied the convents of the town.

Our loss here through the sickness, which was some kind of fever, and was increased through the want of doctors and medicine, was very great, cartloads of the dead being carried out of the town every day for interment in the ground kept for the purpose outside the fortifications. I recovered sufficiently after about six weeks to be able to get out a little on the ramparts, and there a fearful spectacle often met my gaze, for the dead were brought out of the convents completely naked, and after they had been pitched into carts like so many pieces of wood, were carried out and put into holes scarcely large enough to admit of such a number. This unpleasant office of burying the dead fell chiefly on the Portuguese convicts, and it was surprising to see with what readiness these men went to work. They carried one body at a time, having the legs over their shoulders, and the head dangling down behind them, and when they came to the graves, on account of the piece of ground appropriated for the burials being so small, they had to pack their burdens with the greatest nicety. This sight soon cured me, as I thought what a narrow escape I had had of being handled by these same men; and I was glad to get back to my regiment at Badajoz as soon as possible.

Thus ended the proceedings of 1809. Sir Arthur Wellesley was, after the battle of Talavera, raised to the rank of Viscount Wellington.

CHAPTER 8

The Battle of Busaco

At the beginning of 1810 we proceeded from Badajoz to Olivencia, and were there billeted on the inhabitants, two or more in a house, as the circumstances would permit. I remember one very curious thing which occurred at this time, which was that the names of the drum-majors of the three regiments that were collected in this place were Sun, Moon, and Star, our regiment having the Moon, the Fifty-third the Sun, and the Ninth the Star, so that if having the Sun, Moon, and Star fighting for us was any help, they were there all ready.

I happened to be billeted with a comrade of the name of Lewis Phillips, a Welshman, in a house occupied by a respectable but poor man and his wife, whom we found on the whole very kindly meaning towards us. Their occupation was that of labourers, and at this particular season of the year they were employed in picking olive-berries. Before going out to their work in the morning they would prepare their supper; which, as it was then Lent, and they were not allowed to eat meat, consisted, as far as I was able to observe, of a mixture of greens, oil, cayenne pepper, and salt, which they would leave on the embers in an earthenware jar to be cooked by the time they came back; and as generally either myself or my comrade was in the way, they would ask us to occasionally give it a stir. One day after I had been there some little time, I was left as cook, and feeling in rather a mischievous mood, I cut some of my meat up very small—not much indeed, as may be supposed, out of the pound, which was all that we then received—and put it into the jar;

and by night-time it was so boiled and stirred that even I, who knew it was there, could scarcely recognize it On their return they were very hungry and soon partook of their *caldo,* as they called it, pronouncing it to be very good, and praising me as the best cook they had had for some time, little suspecting what that same best cook had put into it I was foolish enough, though indeed I did not expect what a bother I should throw up, to ask them then what they thought was in their *caldo,* and when I told them there was meat in it, they exclaimed they had eaten the Devil, or words to that effect in their language, which we were beginning to understand pretty well by that time after being so long in the country. When they had been and got rid of all they had eaten for supper, they reported me to their priest for making them eat meat in Lent contrary to the laws of their religion; and on the priest coming to the house he condemned me for ever, and prayed to them telling them not to take any notice, as it was done against their will and by an ignorant Protestant.

They never liked me much afterwards, nor set me to watch their *caldo,* and, as they were obliged to have me there still, managed to make me rather uncomfortable; but this did not altogether debar me from continuing my jokes, and more as I thought it was pretty well time for Lewis to have his turn of it. It happened that Lewis particularly disliked olive oil, and I was myself very fond of it, and as we were very seldom on duty together, it used to fall to the one off to cook and bring the other his meals to the guard. So one day I pitched upon a plan by which to take Mr. Taffy in, he being on guard and I the cook that day. I asked him what he would have for his dinner, and he said some potatoes fried in butter, a piece of bread, and his usual pint of wine: so I got some olive oil, and fried the potatoes in that instead of in butter; and when his turn came for him to be relieved for a time off sentry, took his meal to him, which, coming as it did when he was very hungry, he was not long in lapping up. I then asked him how he had enjoyed it; and he answered he had never had a better meal in his life. I said, "Lewis, I thought you did not like oil." "No, no more I do; there was no oil there." I told him I had fried the potatoes in oil, but I could not make him believe it, so at last I said if he was agreeable I would make another mess in the same manner when we were both together at liberty. He consented, so the first time we were both together to dinner I commenced my frying, he being witness to the whole operation, and I found that I succeeded better in my experiment with Lewis than with the worthy people of the house, for after that he could eat as much oil as I could.

After we had stayed at Olivencia for some weeks, chiefly in order to refresh ourselves after the long and tedious marches, warfare, and illness to which for the last two years we had been subjected, Lord Wellington removed his headquarters to Visen, and the army went for the most part into cantonments on the valley of the Mondego. Lord Wellington knew that his troops were then only strong enough for defensive operations, and was therefore determined, unless strongly reinforced, not to take rash measures; but on the enemy's fresh invasion of Portugal he again shifted his headquarters to Celorico. After that we moved on to another small place, called, as far as I am able to remember, Guarda, near Almeida, about eight or ten leagues from Ciudad Rodrigo.

Almeida was at that time garrisoned by some Portuguese troops commanded by an English officer. The French had invested it, but Lord Wellington expected that it would have been able to baffle the enemy until the commencement of the rainy season, and would thus retard the enemy's movements. Almeida was a town of very great strength, but Massena opened fire on it about the 23rd of August, and it was obliged to capitulate as soon afterwards as the 27th, a magazine containing most of the ammunition having blown up, taking with it great part of the town and the fortifications; the governor being thus disappointed of his desire to detain the French any longer. In this sad accident hundreds of the inhabitants and the soldiery, with many of the enemy, who were assembled outside to watch the effect, were launched into eternity either by the explosion itself or by the huge falling masses. And not only did this misfortune occur, but Ciudad Rodrigo meanwhile had fallen into the enemy's hands, and thus a way was opened for a fourfold contest

Owing to these repeated disappointments of Lord Wellington's plans, we were again obliged to fall back into the valley of the Mondego, crossing that river and taking up our position on the heights of Busaco, situate about six leagues north-east of Coimbra. Our march was one of great difficulty, owing to the heavy rains and bad roads, but Lord Wellington did his best to provide against these as much as possible by taking the best road; while, on the other hand, Massena, who was following us up on his way to Lisbon, had taken the very worst; and what was more, owing to ignorance of the country, had little expected to meet a range of heights with, above all, us on the top of them, ready to retard his progress as much as possible.

We arrived at Busaco about the centre of September, and on the 26th our line was formed. Our division, under General Cole, occupied the extreme left of the line, looking down on a flat country, where the British cavalry were drawn up in reserve. The divisions of Generals Hill, Leith, and Picton occupied the right of our line, with the first division, commanded by Sir Bryant Spencer, in the centre. In the meantime the French had taken up their position in front, and a splendid view we had of their encampment from Busaco heights for a time; but it was not destined to be for long that we were to witness this fine sight, without mingling some of their best blood with ours, for early on the morning of the 27th they were in active stir, evidently in the full intention of storming our heights. We were immediately ordered under arms, and ready, if necessary, to go into action.

Early in the morning the French made their appearance. The action commenced on our right and centre, the heaviest fire keeping there the whole time that the battle lasted, as the division I was in had but slight brushes with them. The French must have lost in this engagment some four or five thousand men, while we lost little more than a thousand: but it must be borne in mind what an immense advantage we had over them, as, being situated as we were on the heights, we could witness their every movement That night they retreated to their old position, disheartened at the little success they had gained, or rather at the actual defeat they had suffered, and not feeling inclined to renew the contest next day: and some very slight engagements were all that ensued, chiefly on the left where the light infantry were.

Whilst strolling about one day on these heights I caught a fine cock, which I tamed by tying him to my knapsack by the leg and carrying him about with me, much to the amusement of my comrades; for after I had had him about a fortnight, he became so tame that he would sit on my knapsack quite quietly, without even the string to his leg. We named him Tom, and I took to carrying him about everywhere, even on to the battle-field, wherever my knapsack went, Tom went too, and when the balls were whizzing about, which he did not seem altogether to like, he would make that curious noise which many may have observed as such which a bird like this would make when pursued or frightened. He served, however, to while away many a long and dreary hour pleasantly by his peculiar little ways, and we all became very fond of him: and he grew quite fat on the many tit-bits he received from my comrades and myself during our mess, it being quite marvellous to see how regularly he went to each in turn for his contribution. And it was still more curious to see how Tom was always ready for action on any move of the knapsacks, and not only that, but how very seldom he made any mistake as to which was the right one. However, certain it was that after he had inhabited my knapsack for a little time he had made sufficient marks on it that I could never mistake it for any other, so perhaps he went by them as well as myself.

CHAPTER 9

The Lines of Torres Vedras

On Lord Wellington finding that the French intended to alter their route, and so escape this formidable height, he retreated towards Lisbon himself, passing Coimbra, at which place the Portuguese took some thousands of the French sick and wounded, together with some few effective troops, who had been left to protect the hospital. From Coimbra we proceeded farther south, having again to cross the Mondego, which we did in the latter end of September, reaching Leiria on the 2nd of October.

On the march we passed a nunnery, where we halted for about a quarter of an hour. A great many of the nuns were crowding the balconies to watch us, and as the French were following us up pretty close, the colonel ordered the doors to be broken open by a body of grenadiers, which was soon done, myself being among the number told off for the purpose. This was not carried out, however, without an accident, for one of the women meanwhile fell from a balcony, owing to the crowded state in which they were packed on it. The poor women seemed very glad to get their liberty, for they came out as thick as a flock of sheep, and a great many of them soon passed us bound for Lisbon, being fearful of consequences if they took any other direction: as the French were after us so near as to skirmish with our rear-guard, which chiefly consisted of cavalry.

Lord Wellington had indeed issued a proclamation ordering all the inhabitants to fall back on the approach of the enemy, and destroy any articles that they might possess and were not able to carry with them, that were at all likely to be of any use to the enemy; and so thousands of the population of the country that seemed about to fall within the bounds of the enemy's marches were to be seen, flying from their dwellings, and our army during its retreat was accompanied by crowds of miserable men, women, and children, all eager to reach the capital, as they knew that if they fell in with the French, they would be treated as some had been before, with all the barbarities of an atrocious enemy. I have often heard talk of "moving" in England, and have seen a cart or wagon with a man driving a load of furniture, at the rate of three miles an hour, with a woman and perhaps several children sitting on the top, or at the back, but I never before or since saw such a wholesale move as this was, for every one seemed anxious to carry as many of his effects as he could find room for. The farther we proceeded the more confused our retreat appeared, for multitudes were obliged to rest weary and exhausted by the roadside, and often, though made eager in their endeavours as they heard of the enemy's approach to again renew their tedious journey, were found dying or even dead from their hard exertions, and the road was everywhere strewn with pieces of all kinds of furniture, which the poor fugitives had vainly attempted to get forward.

From Leiria we went on further to Torres Vedras, which we gained after a long, tedious, and impressive march, and there we took up our position at some fine breastworks which Lord Wellington had for some time previous ordered to be thrown up by the Portuguese peasantry in case of the retreat of our army Now we found how much we needed them, for on the 10th of October the French came in sight of our strong position, where we had drawn up, determined that they should not proceed one step farther towards Lisbon.

Massena was rather surprised at our strength, which was quite unexpected by him. He had thought of driving the English into the sea, but he now found his mistake, so encamped about a mile and a half from our position.

On the 14th, however, he attacked our lines near Sobral, but was repulsed; and on another occasion a slight skirmish took place on the right of the line, in which the French general, St.

Croix, was killed by the fire from our gunboats; but on account of our strong position, the French did not come to a general engagement.

The cold and rainy weather having now set in, Lord Wellington had provided as well as possible for the best reception of his troops, who were mostly now in cantonments, whilst those of Massena's army were subject to hardships of the worst description, owing to the cold, wet, and above all insufficient food and raiment, for .they were far away from all supplies from their own country, and there were guerillas or mountain rebels always on the watch to intercept such as were sent, while our army was so near Lisbon that it could always get abundance. Our regiment was situated in a village called Patamara, in the front of our works, where we lay as comfortably as if we had been living in peaceful times; though we were so near the enemy that we very often wandered into the same vineyards, and exchanged compliments by shaking hands.

We were cantoned in a large cellar, but it was unfortunately empty, or at least there was no wine in it, and though there was a quantity of wheat in a vat, we had no need of that, as we had plenty of our own supplies. The owner of our cellar generally visited us every day, and we could not help thinking after a time that he seemed to take particular notice of a large box or bin that two of our men were using to sleep in, so we moved it one morning, and found that the ground underneath had been disturbed. Of course we thought that there must be some treasure concealed there, so we went to work with our bayonets, having no other tools at hand, and soon we came across a large jar, which we found contained bags of dollars, about two hundred and fifty in each bag; which treasure we distributed privately among the cellar company, carefully breaking the jar and returning the earth to its proper place, with the chest on the top of it, so that a minute eye could not have told that it had been disturbed.

Next morning as usual the owner came, bringing with him two labourers, who set to work filling the chest with wheat from the vat, evidently with the intention of making it weighty,

54

he little suspecting that his treasure, which he supposed was underneath, had been divided amongst his tenants. After that we thought we were pretty right from detection, but we were mistaken, for in the morning our restless owner again made his appearance with the two labourers. I should think that that night he must have dreamt of our manoeuvre, for he now shifted the wheat back again into its place, moved the chest, and raised the earth and the broken jar, but found the bird had flown. I shall never forget the rage the man was in. I thought he would have torn the hair off his head; in fact, he did tear some up by the roots, but he must have found that a poor way of showing his spite. He cried, "*Ladrone! Ladrone!*" which was his way of expressing "Thief! Thief!" but finding that we did not take much notice of him, he reported his loss to the colonel, or rather went off to him with that intention; but as the colonel did not understand his language, I was sent for, as by that time I was pretty well acquainted with it; and on my replying to the question as to what the Portuguese wanted, that he required a corporal and three privates to guard a stack of wood, the colonel told me to let him know that he had nothing to do with it I told the Portuguese that it was no use his making a noise about the money, as it must have been only a little change that he could not conveniently recover, unless he could bring proper witnesses to prove he had put the money there.

That only appeased him for the night, however, for he came bothering the colonel again next morning. The colonel again sent for me and asked me what on earth this man wanted now, so I was then obliged to admit the truth. I asked him if he would forgive me for telling him an untruth overnight, and on his consenting, I told him the Portuguese had lost a quantity of money, which he put down at seven thousand dollars. The Portuguese's answer to the question who had placed the money there was that he had himself, but he could bring no witnesses to show that he had really done it, so the colonel said he could have nothing to do with the affair. However, the following morning the plague again appeared, so the colonel to quiet him told him that the grenadiers had some prize money which was expected in a few days, and which he should receive in lieu of what he had lost, which sent the old man off seemingly as satisfied as if he had already got the money in his possession, shaking hands with us all round, and bowing and scraping as if we had been so many kings.

The matter did not altogether rest here, however, for the colonel suspecting that we were implicated, next day we were ordered as if for marching, just as if we were going to leave the place that very day, but the men being quite up to that trick, knowing that the French were still in front, concealed their shares of the money in and around the cellar. I remember well the manner in which my own and one of my fellow-comrades' shares were hidden: there was a heap of pumpkins in the cellar, and in one of these we enclosed our money, cutting a piece out of it of sufficient size to admit the dollars, and after closing it up with the top of the original piece, mixing it again with the remainder of the heap. The company was then marched out into a field, and all our knapsacks and pockets were searched, but even the little money that some must have had before was missing.

The colonel did not mind being baffled so much as the major did, who told the colonel that if he left it in his hands he would endeavour to find the money, to which the colonel replied that he was just the man the Portuguese wanted. The manner in which this cunning major went to work might have succeeded with men less artful than he found us to be, but every one in the cellar had part in it, so it was to the interest of all to keep the affair secret, and not only that, but every man's share in the prize happened to amount to more than the sum which the major offered to any one who would reveal it He came to one of the sergeants of the grenadiers and told him to pick out ten of the men who would be most likely to inform, but instead of doing so, I think the sergeant must have chosen the ten worst rogues in the company. These were then all marched off to the major's quarters, and had in one by one to see him, as he sat with five guineas lying on his table, which he offered to the first who should reveal the mystery. but finding, after he had interviewed about three of them, that he was being duped, for they all told the same tale, that was that they knew nothing about the money, he was so enraged that he told them all to go about their business, saying that they were all a set of thieves, and next time he saw the colonel he had to own, much to the amusement both of the latter and of the whole regiment, that he had been beaten in his knowing undertaking.

Massena remained a little more than a month in his position in front of Torres Vedras, when, owing to want of food and ammunition, he was compelled to retrace his steps, not being able to get supplies through Spain, as the guerillas—who were the most warlike and independent race of the Spaniards, being chiefly offenders who had escaped to the mountains and there formed themselves into one strong body amounting to some thousands—were always on the watch for any supplies that they might catch hold of, more especially from the enemy, and appropriate to their own use. Much credit is due to Lord Wellington for thus drawing the enemy to a place such as Torres Vedras, where they could get no supplies, and further, could gain no advantage, but on the other hand must have lost some thousands through want, cold and wet

From Torres Vedras Massena's army proceeded to Santarem, about ten leagues from Torres Vedras, and there took up his position on the Tagus, whence foraging parties were sent out to scour the country for provisions, who committed horrible excesses on the inhabitants, carrying away their cattle, or any provisions they could lay their hands on. It was this that chiefly infuriated the inhabitants against the French, and caused them to retaliate on any of their stragglers or wounded whom they came across butchering and using them in a most awful manner; and even then, after all this work, this method of gathering provisions for so large an army as Massena's was soon exhausted.

When the French had retreated from Torres Vedras, Lord Wellington left some troops in charge of his lines there, and followed to Santarem, but no general battle took place, only small engagements. The enemy seemed pretty firm to their ground, so Lord Wellington moved his army into cantonments again. Our detachment was lying some distance from Santarem on the Tagus; the actual name of the place is blotted from my memory by lapse of years.

It was rather curious that while there we received our South American prize money; money taken from the very people we were now allied with, so that a great part of it was spent amongst them again. Each private received eight dollars, and I believe the sergeants sixteen.

The Lisbon traders must have got scent of this, for a quantity of boats laden with little requisites and luxuries ascended the river from Lisbon to trade amongst the soldiers, and so we were soon enabled to rid ourselves of our little spare cash. Our colonel was very considerate to these people, and being determined as far as possible to prevent all plunder, had their boats or stalls guarded by sentries. This, however, did not altogether hinder some of the more daring from getting things on the cheap now and then, but they were so trifling that they are hardly worthy of mention.

CHAPTER 10
Ordered to Badajoz

The remainder of the year 1810 was spent in these cantonments, the French still lying in their position at Santarem. But the beginning of 1811 brought on us more and fatal work, for Soult's army had invested Olivencia and Badajoz, and obliged them, not being garrisoned by the British, but only by the Spaniards, to surrender. The way was thus paved for one of the worst engagements in the whole Peninsular war; I mean the storming of Badajoz.

The French did not move from Santarem till the beginning of March, which we discovered on the 6th, and Lord Wellington, having received fresh reinforcements from England, determined on following them up. They had taken three routes, and consequently our army had to be divided too. Our division, which was the Fourth, with the First and Sixth divisions, commanded by Marshal Beresford, was to follow by way of Thomar, and the main body of the army by way of Leiria and Pombal, and so again to unite.

On our route we came up with the French at Thomar, but on our appearance they retreated to Espinal, a short distance off Pombal, and took up a strong position between these two latter places. We followed them up and combined ourselves again into one body. At Pombal the French had tried, but in vain, to retain the old castle situated there, and some slight skirmishing had taken place between them and some of our light troops. At Redinha the third, fourth, and light divisions attacked the enemy's left, and after a stout engagement we compelled them to retire upon their main body, and being likewise attacked on the right, their whole body was thrown into retreat on Condexo. On our appearance there, they set fire to the place, and again retreated; their object in burning such a little town being probably to prevent our cavalry, cannon, and ammunition from following them up too closely. We were, however, delayed but a very short time, for we marched through the burning town, certainly not letting the grass grow under our feet, as the ground was much too hot. It appeared once to have been a beautiful town, but after this it was one sad mass of ruin.

The French proceeded from this place to Casal Nova, but were so quickly followed up that Picton's division overtook them and nearly captured their leader. Next day we came up with the enemy, posted in a strong position at Casal Nova, and on the 14th of March the light division attacked them and obliged them to retreat to a neighbouring height, whence after another attack they again found it best to retire on Miranda de Corno. Part of our division was in this engagement, and I never saw cannon play with better or more deadly effect on any body of men than ours did on the enemy, situated as they were on the heights of Casal Nova. Yet they left very few dead or wounded on the field; I think they must have carried most of them away, as the ground was strewn with muskets and swords.

The thing I noticed most particularly in this fight was the singular death of a man in our regiment, who was named William Halfhead, but considering the size of his head, which must have gone a very great way towards filling half a bushel measure, it was wrongly so, and he was the sport of the whole regiment, who named him Bushelhead. His head was indeed so large that he had to have two caps to make him one. This poor fellow was standing within five yards of me when a shot from the enemy's cannon took this same head clean off. I heard one of the men exclaim, "Hullo, there goes poor Bushelhead," and that was all the sympathy he got.

One division, under General Cole, proceeded after the enemy to Panella, where it was joined by another, under General Nightingale, and on the enemy seeing how closely they were followed they retreated from Miranda de Corno, setting fire to that town also. We again fell in with them on the banks of a river near the village of Poz de Aroce, where a brisk attack was made on them by the British, and they were driven from the river in great confusion with a loss of some four hundred men or more. It has been reported that numbers were even killed by their own side, through the darkness of the night and the confusion arising from their not having expected an attack then.

We encamped there one day, and then again pursued the enemy, coming up with them where they were posted behind the river Alva. There they had sent out four or five hundred foragers in search of provisions: and indeed they must have wanted them badly, for even we that had come from the land of plenty at Torres Vedras were at that time in great want We did not, however, let them stay there long enough for the suppliers to return, for we opened fire on them, and forced them to retreat to Moira, leaving their foraging parties to the mercy of the English and Portuguese, most of them sooner or later falling into our hands. We crossed the Alva on a floating bridge and halted near Moira, as the enemy had now retreated to Celorico; but here Lord Wellington was obliged to stay the pursuit through want of provisions.

On hearing of the state of Badajoz he had already determined to send reinforcements to that place, so our division and one of the Portuguese under General Hamilton, with a brigade of cavalry, were directed to march southward again and invest Badajoz before that place's defences could be repaired by the enemy. Accordingly, on the 17th of March, our divisions crossed the Tagus at Tancos, whence we advanced to Portalegre, halting there for about two days.

Here I think I ought to relate an incident just to show that the English often committed depredations on the inhabitants almost as bad as the enemy. We are often too prone to see other people's and nations' faults, whilst if our own had but the light thrown on them, they would often come up to, if not exceed, those of our adversaries.

We, at least my company, were billeted in a chapel, at night lying on straw, which in the morning had to be rolled up neatly in our blankets so as to make the place look comfortable during the day, a separate lot of straw being allowed for every two men. Very close to this chapel there was situated a farmyard, inhabited by a quantity of pigs: and pork being a thing which the company had not tasted for some time, we made up our minds to have a treat So one of our number was chosen to steal a pig, being, I suppose, one whose fingers were thought well adapted to the purpose. He pitched on a very novel plan of proceeding, for, taking a sergeant's pike, he stuck the pig with it, and then escaped till the poor animal had died; on which, not being long afterwards, we conveyed it to the chapel.

We thought that we had done this all unobserved, but the farmer had either watched our movements, or must have seen the blood and gone to count, and so missed the pig, and we soon saw that all was not to pass off so nicely as we expected, for presently he put in an appearance at the chapel too. Finding, however, that we were too strong for him, and seeing nothing of the missing pig, he went off and reported the circumstance to our colonel.

Meanwhile we lost no time in making our plans for a place of security for our prize. At first we thought of our straw beds, that is, of wrapping the pig in the blanket, but our afterthoughts told us that that would not be safe. At one end of the chapel, however, there was a large statue of the Virgin Mary, having on a robe with a long train, and it was under this train that we concealed our prize in the best possible manner, so as to baffle any chance of detection by the appearance of the train being altered. And sure enough, it proved to be the safest place we could have hit upon for our desired end, for very soon in came the farmer with a priest, and the first thing they did wos to make their obedience to the monument, whilst we were all the time laughing in our sleeves to think how they were likewise honouring the pig.

Something more serious was soon to happen, however, for a very few minutes afterwards the captain and colonel both came in and ordered every berth to be examined; but they searched in vain, and pronounced it to be some mistake on the farmer's part, as in that short time we could not have cooked, eaten, or otherwise got rid of the pig. The farmer, however, still felt certain that we had it, but it could not be found anywhere in the chapel, so he was obliged to retire without any compensation for his unfortunate pig. Then we breathed a little more freely at last, for if we had been found out, we most likely should have had our grog stopped for some time, and that goes in such times very much against the heart of a soldier.

Early next morning our kettles were at work in the usual way, cooking our breakfasts, but that particular morning every man of the chapel company had a small extra portion in the pot, being his allowance of the pig, not much certainly, when it came to be divided amongst so many, about one pound for each man; but even that, and the more especially as it was pork, was thought no little of in such times of short diet, for we were not over abundantly stocked with provisions. In fact it was chiefly for that reason, and to refresh ourselves from the long continued marches, that we were now delaying on our southward route.

On again resuming our march, we arrived in four or five days at a place called Campo Mayor, where we caught sight of the enemy, but only in marching order towards Badajoz. Here I have again to relate another shameful instance of plunder which happened on the same march. We were encamped near a village of no particular note, and of which therefore I did not arrive at the exact name: and a party of men, perhaps to the number of about twenty, including myself, were out on the forage, when we arrived at the house of a poor woman, who evidently kept a kind of general shop, though we could not see any other houses near. Four or five with myself went into the shop and asked the woman if she had any bread for sale, to which she replied that there was some baking which would be done in about an hour, if we could wait, which we consented to do; but meanwhile a signal was given to the remaining part of our company, who, observing that the oven was built out from the house, immediately set to work to make a hole with their bayonets so as to be able to get the bread out. While this operation was going on out at the back we were amusing the woman with some of our Peninsular tales in front until the hour had passed; when, on her going to draw the bread she found much to her amazement that every loaf was missing, and daylight gleaming in on her through a hole in the back of the oven. The poor woman was then in a terrible stew, and we did all we could to reconcile her to her loss, making out that we knew nothing of the sad business; but this pity did not detain us long, for we pretty quickly made for the camp and made a first rate meal off the bread, which was to us then a greater luxury than meat, as we were very seldom supplied with bread, more especially so fresh as this, which was smoking hot, though not very well done; but if it had been dough we could have eaten it at that time.

On another occasion, on the same march, I caught another cock, or rather took it from a farm-yard; but not feeling inclined to be troubled with a second live one, as I had still got Tom campaigning with me, I gave it three swings by the head, which I thought broke its neck, and put it away out of sight in my high cap. On my return to camp, the company had just fallen in on parade, and no sooner had the captain passed close to me, than my cap-tenant crew, or made a terrible noise of some sort, much to the astonishment both of myself and the captain, who said, "Hullo, Lawrence, what have you got there?" I told him a cock, which I had bought when out foraging. "Yes," he said, "you offered four, but took it with five," meaning, I suppose, my fingers. He was perfectly right, but I did not think it would have passed off quite so smoothly, as many in the Peninsula were hanged for plunder; all we were allowed to forage for at this place being provisions for the horses and mules.

CHAPTER 11

Badajoz & Albuera

From Campo Mayor we went on towards Badajoz, some slight skirmishing with the enemy's rearguard taking place on the way, but with very little success on either side. We made a stay at Elvas until preparations had been made for crossing the Guadiana, and then we proceeded to Badajoz, the town that so pestered the Allies during the Peninsular War. Our brigade took up its position on the north side of the town and river, and commenced throwing up batteries. During our operations the French sallied out of the town, crossed the river, and attempted to destroy a part of our work, thus actively engaging about three hundred of our covering party, together with a small reinforcement of grenadiers, which latter, however, soon made them beat a retreat into the town again.

I succeeded in capturing a straggler here, but was not able to get him into our lines by myself, on account of his lying down and refusing to come; so I broke his musket, but not feeling inclined even then to leave him, I knelt down to protect myself a little from the enemy's shot, and waited for some assistance. This was not long in coming, for the colonel, seeing my position, allowed a man, Towser by name, who had volunteered, to come and lend me a hand, and thus we were enabled to get my captive safe at last to the lines: not, however, without some risk to our own lives, as the enemy were firing at us all the time from a fort situated a short distance from the river. The man was not at all willing at first to walk, so we dragged him by the leg along the ground for some way; but owing to the roughness of the road, he soon found that he preferred walking. We searched him and found a doubloon and a half on his person, which Towser and I divided equally between us. The colonel reprimanded me for running such a risk for one prisoner, but he was satisfied with my answer, which was that perhaps the man had been on the alert to fire at some of us, which might have terminated in the colonel's own death, or maybe in mine. The colonel had already been slightly wounded in the leg, which obliged him afterwards to go into the hospital at Elvas, and some thirty-eight of my comrades unfortunately met their deaths in this affray.

The colonel sent a quantity of rum from Elvas to be divided amongst those men who were in action at the time he received his wound, but the officer then in charge of us, whom nobody in the regiment liked, only served out the half of it, which only came to about half a pint for each man, much to the discontent of all. I spoke out and said that we ought to have it all, as the colonel had sent it, and we had had to fight hard for it; which so put out the officer that he said I should not have any at all. The sergeant, however, gave me a half a pint with the rest, unbeknown to the officer, and immediately went and asked him if I was to have any. The officer then told him to "let the rascals have the lot, and then they would be satisfied," so thus I came in for another half pint, which I put into my canteen with some water to drink when I might next be on sentry.

This came to my turn on the very night following, and as it chanced, I was commanded by the same officer that I have been alluding to. It was not often that the major went round with the picket, but that night, having taken the colonel's command, he did so, and saw me placed on sentry. I was placed as outlying sentry, and ought to have been relieved in three hours, instead of which, out of spite for the rum job, the officer never came near me all night; in fact, I never saw a man from the time I was put on till I came off myself in the morning. I will give some details of the coincidences of that night, which was dark but starlight, so that I could just catch a dim glimpse of the enemy's before mentioned fort, and, owing to the heights, was able to see the town very well.

The place where I was on sentry was in a field of standing wheat in ear, amongst which I sat down and was fairly comfortable for about an hour; after which the enemy seemed to have made out my position, and kept dabbing at me with their muskets for a long time. I could not make out how it was they had caught sight of me, but after they had continued firing for some time, I at last found out the cause. On my cap there was a large bright brass plate, which no doubt made a slight reflection either from the stars or the light from the town, and so drew their attention to me. So much for bright dress and brass plates, thought I, though fortunately they had done me no harm; and now for the remedy that I proposed. I took the loading-rod from my musket, and stuck it fast into the ground, and placing my cap upon it, I proceeded about ten yards to the right and sat down; and it was fortunate that I did so, for during the night they put two shots through my cap, and that would have been awkward if my head had been inside. It is not to be supposed, however, that I sat there bareheaded all night, for I put on my slop or foraging cap, and then sat hearkening to the sound of chimes and bells pronouncing the hours of eleven, twelve, one, two, three, and four, and the occasional whizzing of shells and shot over my head.

At length, after hearing the bells strike the last-named hour, and seeing the dawn, too, beginning to peep over the distant horizon, knowing that my turn to be relieved had long since passed, I put back my loading rod into its place and my cap on my head, and decamped to the body picket. There I met the major, who seeing me return, and knowing that it was my turn for rest, asked me where I had been. I said, "Were you not with the officer when he placed me on sentry last night?" He replied; "Yes, has he not relieved you since?" On which I told him no, and that I thought it was time to relieve myself, likewise showing him my cap for him to judge what a hot night I had had of it I also gave the reason that I thought for the officer's spite, which put him out terribly, so much so that he immediately called up the officer, who had retired to rest some hours, and told him that if they had not been so near the enemy, he would have had him tried by court-martial for his neglect: which might have ended by his being cashiered out of the service. That was the first and last time that he ever left me on sentry all night.

Our stay here, however, was of short duration for we proceeded further towards Olivencia, which was garrisoned by about four hundred of the enemy. We crossed the Guadiana near that place on a bridge constructed of empty casks and planks, and sat down before the town about the 11th of April. In a few days our batteries were all ready for action, and on the garrison refusing to surrender, we commenced firing, and soon made a breach; but at that point the governor, fearing an assault, immediately surrendered, and he and his garrison were all taken prisoners.

It was at this place that I parted with Tom. For being bothered by the colonel's servant to let him have my pet, I foolishly consented, though my comrades did their best to persuade me to keep him. He told me he wanted to take him to England, and gave me a dollar for him, but I afterwards found out that he had killed him for his master's dinner. I think I felt as sorry for that as I ever did for anything, for I dearly liked Tom.

From Olivencia we marched again towards Badajoz, but owing to Soult's army being on its way to relieve that town, Beresford had occupied the heights of Albuera, about thirteen miles south-east of Badajoz, in order to check the enemy if possible in their intended object. General Cole therefore advanced to Albuera as well, and the action had just commenced when he arrived. The Allies had taken up their position on a fine ridge of heights, and the French under Marshal Soult made their appearance on the 15th of May.

On the following morning they made an attack on the right, which was occupied by the Spaniards, who soon gave way in great disorder, again leaving the brunt of the battle to the British; and not only that, but also thus allowing the French to gain part of the heights. A noble attack, however, was made by the Second division, the first brigade of which in trying to gain the ridge was met by the fierce Polish Lancers, who slaughtered a tremendous number of them; in fact, the battle was at one time thought to have been gained by the French, and most likely would have been, had not Colonel Harding hurled part of our division and a reserve Portuguese brigade against the enemy, and so renewed the fight. General Cole himself led our fusiliers up the hill. Six British guns and some colours were then already in the enemy's possession, but Cole's troops soon dispersed the lancers, and, recapturing the guns and colours, drove the French down again in confusion.

It is useless for me to give any further details of this celebrated battle, for it has been already depicted so many times and so much more ably than I could do; but the Allies could not have lost less than seven thousand killed, wounded and missing, while the French loss was stated to be nine thousand. It was seldom, however, that we arrived at the correct estimate of the enemy's loss, it being generally the custom to state it as greater than ours,and my opinion is that in this battle the Allies lost quite an equal number to the French. The Spaniards especially must have sustained a great loss in their confusion. It was always a bother to get them to stir forward during a battle, but retreating was what they were best at, and then it was always in confusion; at the battle of Albuera indeed whilst they were in this state they even fired at random, and several shots went amongst the English.

General Cole was himself wounded in this engagement, which resulted so sadly for both parties; for it could hardly be termed a victory for either side, and if so it was a very dearly bought one. Still it was we who remained on the field in the end.

CHAPTER 12

Ciudad Rodrigo

For the remaining part of the year 1811 both armies were inactive. The batteries had been at work at Badajoz and breaches had been made, but these had proved impracticable, twelve forlorn hopes and storming parties having advanced into them with no better result than that many met their deaths and the remainder had to withdraw owing to obstacles. The siege was therefore converted into a blockade, and Lord Wellington, who after taking Almeida and driving the French out of Portugal, had come southward with two divisions to reinforce Beresford's army, moved the general South Army into cantonments and encampments near the River Caza, a tributary of the Guadiana. There we remained till July, when we were marched northward again across the Tagus, and took up our position at Guinaldo. While there no particular engagement ensued; the enemy indeed falling on another part of our line, but no success being obtained on either side.

Although Lord Wellington had now driven the French clean out of Portugal, he had still other work to do; work that praised him more than he had been before, work that raised him to higher honours than he yet possessed, but likewise work that sacrificed more thousands of human beings than had been through the whole three years. There can be no doubt that if he had had as many troops as the French, he would long before this have driven them out of Portugal and perhaps Spain as well; he seemed to understand their every movement, and was thus always ready waiting to receive them; and they on their part seemed to think they had more than found their match in him, and had become very cautious in contending with him. But he actually had only half their number, or even less, that he could depend on, and these were sometimes not fit for service from want or other privations, as these tales of the hospitals or rather deadly convents go to prove, where so many of my comrades passed the end of their lives, and their remains were carried out with no more ceremony than I described as at Elvas.

The Portuguese themselves were mostly exempt from the actual slaughter, but their country had already been left by the enemy in about as bad a state as it could; for if it had been infested with swarms of locusts, the devastation could not have been paralleled. The war could not have left one family quite untouched by its destructiveness or by misery and grief irrecoverable for many years; and indeed, in some cases, for ever, for many a child was deprived of its father or mother, or even of both parents, and many were the parents who had lost their children; and if any had accumulated a little fortune then it must have been lost, being ever liable to be plundered by the soldiery.

It must be said, however, that certainly the Spaniards and likewise the Portuguese behaved on their part very cruelly to the enemy's wounded, prisoners, or stragglers. I myself was witness to one of their barbarous acts. They had laid a ring of straw round a wounded Frenchman and set fire to it, and when the poor man tried to crawl out, he was only received with a pitchfork which sent him again into the centre. We soon made the Portuguese fly by firing in amongst them, but when we came up to the poor man, his hair, fingers, and face were fearfully burnt already. He implored us not to leave him, but we were obliged to, and no doubt either the Portuguese returned and killed him, or else he died of the injuries he had sustained at their hands, or from the wounds that had before disabled him.

These barbarities, however, the enemy brought on themselves by dealing out the same coin, for they would go on foraging parties, and perhaps find a whole family or more together trying to protect their very subsistences, when they would kill the males, serve the females not much better, and carry off everything they could lay their hands on if of any value. Sometimes, however, they were overpowered in these freaks, and then they suffered just as bad a fate as I showed just now; which, after all, is not much to be wondered at

I am sorry to say, however, that we ourselves were not quite free from the charge of depredations, though we did not carry them on to the extent of bloodshed. An instance of this in which I was myself mixed up happened during our stay at this very place Guinaldo.

We were quartered nearly twenty in number in two upper rooms of a house, of which the family inhabited the lower part. Our beds, as usual, consisted chiefly of straw. An Irish comrade of ours, by name Harding, whom we named Pig Harding, owing to his always being on the look out for any cheap pieces he could lay hands on, was quartered in the same house, and we had not been there many days before he found about thirty pounds of sausages curled round the bottom of a large earthen jar that contained at least ten or twelve gallons of olive oil, the sausages having evidently been placed there either to keep, or to be out of our sight Pig, however, who was up to many of the Spanish movements, was not long in finding them; he soon had tried the bottom with his bayonet, and found a prize worth fishing for; and he came running into our room carrying the sausages, which owing to their oily state did not fail to leave a trace of their whereabouts. We soon repaired this defect so as not to be noticeable on the floor, which was not kept so clean as it might be, and which our stay there had not improved much, and then we had a fine meal off our sausages, which, to use Pig's own words, "Blood and 'ounds, were good, very" and soon there were very few left

After all in the house had eaten sufficient, the rest were given to some of our comrades in another house, our policy being always to get rid of any plunder as quickly as possible so as to bar detection if it was found out. There were always plenty to help eat it, and in this case every one of the sausages were gone before the woman found out her loss, which was not till next day about dinnertime, when no doubt she expected to cook the family meal off them. The sausages in that country were generally made of cooked meat flavoured with garlic and cayenne pepper, so that they were fit for eating at all times without cooking. When the poor woman found them missing, she soon thought of the right parties as the thieves; and with her fingers all dripping with oil, for she had evidently been feeling for them in the jar, she rushed in crying, "*Ladrone, Ladrone* (you thieves, you thieves), the French are bad enough, but you are worse!" We only laughed at her, so she reported us to our major, who immediately came to our room and said, "Then you are up to your prigging tricks again," and asked the woman how much the sausages were worth. She did not fail to ask enough, for she said sixteen dollars, which he paid at once, saying he would deduct it from our pay.

The major never did as he said he would, however, and we heard no more either of the sausages or of our money; but still we did not know that at the time, and the threat only had the effect of sending Pig off again in search of something that would at least give us the worth of our money. He waited till just before we were going to shift from these quarters, and then he found out a trap-door, through which he got himself hoisted up, and found eight sides of bacon there, with one of which he descended, thinking that would be as much as we could conveniently eat at that place, and so at any rate we had the worth of the sixteen dollars, for this last affair was not found out before we started.

On another occasion, whilst we were at the same place, some Spaniards came into our camp with wine for sale, contained in pigskins carried across mules' backs, one on each side, and whilst the Spaniard was measuring it out of one skin, a hole had been made in the other with a penknife, which lightened both burdens at once considerably, much to the discontent of the Spaniard on finding it out. But I think that all such lesser manoeuvres as this, though bad in themselves, can be perhaps looked over in considering the frequent hungry state that so large a body of men were in during this war.

We remained in this neighbourhood till the latter end of 1811. The beginning of 1812 opened with the siege of Ciudad Rodrigo, where we arrived and began to break ground on the 8th of February.

We had to commence throwing up our batteries and breastworks under a particular annoyance from three guns, situated on a fortified convent a little distance from the town, near where our brigade's operations were in progress, so our colonel for one volunteered to storm the convent, which offer was accepted. Several companies, therefore, including my own, advanced under him unobserved by the enemy in the darkness of the night, and succeeded in effecting an entrance into the convent, the garrison being taken by surprise, but managing to decamp. I then volunteered with a few men to march on up to the tower where the guns were situated, a priest being made to show us the way, as the path which we had to tread was so winding. When we arrived at the top, which must have taken us at least ten minutes, we found no French there, but the three shattered cannon still remained, which we were ordered to pitch down, not much improving their condition thereby, and so we gained the object for which we had come. All the French that were left in the convent, or at least all I saw there, were two of their wounded, but they were good enough to leave us a room full of cabbages, which came in very handy.

After this affair we took up our quarters in the convent, but still continued our ground work. Once the enemy sallied out of the town and attacked us during these operations, and a smart brush ensued, but they were soon obliged to retire again. Now and then the garrison would greet us with a cannon-ball, which often did some little mischief, a sergeant was killed by one, which at the same time took another's arm off, and I myself had a narrow escape one day whilst in the breastworks, from a six-pounder which having struck the convent, rebounded and caught me in the chest. Luckily it was nearly spent, but as it was it knocked me down, and it was some time before I could recover my breath, and that not until my comrades had poured some rum and water down my throat My chest was much discoloured and swollen, through which I was ill for nearly a week.

By the 19th of January two practicable breaches were made in the walls of the town, and an attack was ordered. Our colonel volunteered for the forlorn hope, but it was put under other commanders, being chiefly composed of the Rifles. The main breach was committed to General Picton's division, and the brigades of General Vandeleur and Colonel Barnet were ordered to attack the smaller breach, headed by a storming-party of three hundred men and a forlorn hope, under Major George Napier of the Fifty-second regiment. The forlorn hope assembled between seven and eight o'clock under the walls of the convent we were then occupying, which protected them a little from the enemy's shot. All was deathly silent amongst those men, who perhaps could not help thinking that it might be their last undertaking: in fact, this is much the worst business a soldier can enter upon, as. scarcely anything but death looks him in the face. There they were watching with intense anxiety for the to many fatal signal; and at length the order was given to advance.

The assault was to be conducted on all sides at once, and in double quick time the troops were at the breach, although the ladders, which were being carried by the Portuguese, when wanted had disappeared. Our troops nevertheless pushed onwards and gained the breach, when either through accident or the neglect of the train-man, a mine was sprung before the French were clearly off it, and both French and English were suddenly blown into the air and buried together in the ruin. After the smother had fairly cleared away, our troops met with very little difficulty in mounting the breach and scouring the ramparts, the French throwing down their arms and retiring into the town itself, where after a brief contest in the streets, the whole surviving garrison surrendered; but it was not without the loss of many of the bravest men on our side in the first assault.

This successful achievement was attended with all the horrors of the soldiery, excesses, riot, and drunkenness taking place on every side. Houses were plundered of their contents, cellars broken open and emptied, and many houses were even set on fire, amid the yells of the dissipated soldiers and the screams of the wounded. Thus the night passed, but in the morning order was a little restored, and those men who were sensible enough returned to their own regiments.

About forty-one pieces of cannon, some stands of arms, and a quantity of provisions were taken, besides which the enemy must have lost quite a thousand men, besides the prisoners. Amongst these latter were six or seven deserters belonging to the Allied army, who were sent to their respective regiments and probably shot: fortunately there were none belonging to our division. The Allies' loss was very considerable, being upwards of a thousand also. After the reduction of Ciudad Rodrigo, Lord Wellington put it under garrison and ordered the breaches to be repaired. Then he marched south to watch the proceedings at Badajoz, whilst we again went into cantonments near Rodrigo.

Some muleteers halted under the protection of our troops at this place, laden with rum and biscuits for the supply of the army, over which sentries were placed on guard, but instead of guarding, they took so much rum, which being there generally carried in pigs' skins was easily got at, that they died in consequence next morning. Likewise one of our cavalry men was here flogged for making away with his horse's corn to selfishly buy himself grog; and well deserving of punishment he was, for the poor horse was miserably thin. In fact, the horses in general were the same, and it was thought that many were served the same; but this man being the first that was caught, was tried by court-martial and sentenced to fifty lashes as an example. The man asked the colonel to look over it as it was his first offence, but the colonel said, "The horse's looks tell a different tale from that; he has long had the bitters, and you the sweet, and now it is time things should be the other way round." Certainly the horses' forage could not at all times be procured, and especially in the winter, but for that very reason they had more need of it when it could be. The best horses I saw during the whole Peninsular campaign were the German hussars': those men were not so fond of drink as ours, which might perhaps account for the condition of their animals, as they had no more chance of gaining forage than our men had.

Chapter 13

The Forlorn Hope

Our stay at Rodrigo was of short duration, for we were soon ordered south to invest Badajoz, which gave us another long and tedious march of a hundred and fifty miles or more. We arrived there at the beginning of March, and the third, ours, that is the fourth, and the light divisions, under the command of Marshal Beresford and General Picton, invested the town.

We soon broke ground before the town by commencing to throw up breastworks and batteries. Very heavy rains had just lately set in, but our troops still pursued their undertaking and persevered in the trenches. A cannonade was kept up from the town, which fortunately, however, did not do much damage; but on the 19th of March the garrison attacked us, and were only driven back with a loss on our side of a hundred men killed and wounded, and a still greater loss on their part.

I killed a French sergeant myself with my bayonet in this action. I was at the time in the trenches when he came on the top and made a dart at me with his bayonet, having, like myself, exhausted his fire; and while in the act of thrusting he overbalanced himself and fell. I very soon pinioned him to the ground with my bayonet, and the poor fellow soon expired. I was sorry afterwards that I had not tried to take him prisoner instead of killing him, but at the time we were all busily engaged in the thickest of the fight, and there was not much time to think about things. And besides that, he was a powerful-looking man, being tall and stout, with a beard and moustache completely covering his face, as fine a soldier as I have seen in the French army, and if I had allowed him to gain his feet, I might have suffered for it; so perhaps in such times my plan was the best—kill or be killed.

About eight hundred of us were every night busily engaged in the trenches, whilst a large number, who were called the covering party, were on the look out in case of an attack from the enemy. The rain poured down so fast that balers were obliged to be employed in places, and at times the trenches were in such a state of mud that it was over our shoes. We were chiefly employed during the day in finishing off what we had done in the night, as very little else could be done then owing to the enemy's fire. We had not been to work many days before we got within musket shot of a fine fort situated a little distance from the town, and garrisoned with four or five hundred of the enemy, who annoyed us rather during our operations. One night as I was working in the trenches near this place, and just as the guard was about to be relieved, a shell from the town fell amongst them and exploded, killing and wounding about thirty. I never saw a worse sight of its kind, for some had their arms and legs, and some even their heads, which was worse, completely severed from their bodies. I remember my comrade, Pig Harding, who was working near me at the time, and had, like myself, become hardened to the worst of sights during our sojourn in the Peninsula, saying as a joke, "Lawrence, if any one is in want of an arm or a leg he can have a good choice there," little thinking, poor fellow, that soon he would himself be carried out, numbered with the slain. On the morning after this explosion a terrific scene of our mangled comrades presented itself, for their remains strewed the ground in all directions.

Of course our next thought was how to clear ourselves of this troublesome fort. Some suspicions were entertained that it was undermined, so in the dead of night some engineers were sent between it and the town to search for a train, and finding that the earth had been moved, they dug down and round the train and cut it off. Then, on the next night, the Eighty-seventh and Eighty-eighth regiments were ordered up to storm the fort, and succeeded after a brisk action in gaining the place, the most of the garrison escaping into the town. Next morning I entered the fort with the rest, where we found the wounded Frenchmen lying. We relieved their pain a little by giving them some of our rum and water, and then conveyed them to the rear; most of their wounds being bad, evidently from the bayonet, but not mortal.

Owing to the success of taking this fort we were enabled to carry on our works much nearer to the town, and by the beginning of April two batteries were formed within three or four hundred yards of the place: and in about five days, through the effects of our twenty-four pounders, three practicable breaches were made in the walls.

Lord Wellington then ordered the town to be attacked on the night of the 6th, having previously sent to know if it would surrender: and the answer being "No," he asked for the inhabitants to be allowed to quit, as he intended to take the town by assault. In consequence of this some thousands of the inhabitants quitted the city.

A storming-party was selected from each regiment, and each of the third, fourth, and light divisions was told off to a breach. I joined the forlorn hope myself.

Before, however, that I proceed further in my account of this sanguinary affair, I will relate an engagement that myself, Pig Harding, and another of my comrades, George Bowden by name, entered into before we even started on our way, of which the result showed what a blind one it was. Through being quartered at Badajoz after the battle of Talavera, all three of us knew the town perfectly well, and so understood the position of most of the valuable shops: and hearing a report likewise that if we succeeded in taking the place, there was to be three hours' plunder, we had planned to meet at a silversmith's shop that we knew about, poor Pig even providing himself with a piece of wax candle to light us if needed.

But all this was doomed to disappointment. We were supplied with ladders and grass bags, and having received and eaten our rations, and each man carrying his canteen of water, we fell in at half-past eight or thereabouts to wait for the requisite signal for all to advance. During the interval our men were particularly silent: but at length the deadly signal was given, and we rushed on towards the breach.

I was one of the ladder party, for we did not feel inclined to trust to the Portuguese, as we did at Ciudad Rodrigo. On our arriving at the breach, the French sentry on the wall cried out, "Who comes there?" three times, or words to that effect in his own language, but on no answer being given, a shower of shot, canister and grape, together with fire-balls, was hurled at random amongst us. Poor Pig received his death wound immediately, and my other accomplice, Bowden, became missing, while I myself received two small slug shots in my left knee, and a musket shot in my side, which must have been mortal had it not been for my canteen: for the ball penetrated that and passed out, making two holes in it, and then entered my side slightly. Still I stuck to my ladder, and got into the entrenchment. Numbers had by this time fallen but the cry from our commanders being, "Come on, my lads!" we hastened to the breach; but there, to our great surprise and discouragement, we found a *chevaux de frise* had been fixed and a deep entrenchment made, from behind which the garrison opened a deadly fire on us. Vain attempts were made to remove this fearful obstacle, during which my left hand was dreadfully cut by one of the blades of the *chevaux de frise,* but finding no success in that quarter, we were forced to retire for a time.

We remained, however, in the breach until we were quite weary with our efforts to pass it. My wounds were still bleeding, and I began to feel very weak; my comrades persuaded me to go to the rear; but this proved a task of great difficulty, for on arriving at the ladders, I found them filled with the dead and wounded, hanging some by their feet just as they had fallen and got fixed in the rounds. I hove down three lots of them, hearing the implorings of the wounded all the time; but on coming to the fourth, I found it completely smothered with dead bodies, so I had to draw myself up over them as best I could. When I arrived at the top I almost wished myself back again, for there of the two I think was the worse sight, nothing but the dead and wounded lying around, and the cries of the latter, mingled with the incessant firing from the enemy, being quite deafening.

I was so weak myself that I could scarcely walk, so I crawled on my hands and knees till I got out of reach of the enemy's musketry. After proceeding for some way I fell in with Lord Wellington and his staff, who seeing me wounded, asked me what regiment I belonged to. I told him the Fortieth, and that I had been one of the forlorn hope. He inquired as to the extent of my wounds, and if any of our troops had got into the town, and I said "No," and I did not think they ever would, as there was a *chevaux de frise,* a deep entrenchment, and in the rear of them a constant and murderous fire being kept up by the enemy. One of his staff then bound up my leg with a silk handkerchief, and told me to go behind a hill which he pointed out, where I would find a doctor to dress my wounds; so I proceeded on, and found that it was the doctor of my own regiment

Next after me Lieutenant Elland was brought in by a man of the name of Charles Filer, who had seen him lying wounded at the breach with a ball in the thigh, and on his asking him to convey him from the breach, had raised him on his shoulders for that object. But during his march a cannon-ball had taken the officer's head clean off without Filer finding it out on account of the darkness of the night, and the clamour of cannon and musketry mingled with the cries of the wounded. Much it was to Filer's astonishment, then, when the surgeon asked him what he had brought in a headless trunk for, he declared that the lieutenant had a head on when he took him up, for he had himself asked him to take him from the breach, and that he did not know when the head was severed, which must have been done by one of the bullets of which there were so many whizzing about in all directions. Some may doubt the correctness of this story, but I, being myself both a hearer and an eyewitness to the scene at the surgeon's, can vouch for the accuracy of it. Certainly Filer's appearance was not altogether that of composure, for he was not only rather frightened at the fearful exposure of his own body at the breach and across the plain, but he was evidently knocked up, or rather bowed down, by the weight of his lifeless burden, which he must, if he came from the breach, have carried for upwards of half a mile, so that, under these disadvantages, the mistake might easily have been made even by any one of harder temperament than his. But the tale did not fail to spread through the camp, and caused great laughter over Filer, sentences being thrown at him such as "Who carried the man without a head to the doctor?" &c. After Lord Wellington had found it useless to attempt to face the breach with the *chevaux de frise,* he altered his plans of attack. More success had fortunately been achieved in the other breaches, so he withdrew the men from our fatal breach to reinforce the others, but not till at least two thousand had been killed or wounded in this single assault. He had ordered the castle to be attacked, and a quantity of troops had been supplied for the purpose with long ladders, which had been raised against the walls and filled with men, but the enemy showered down a mass of heavy substances, such as trees and large stones, and amongst all a number of deadly bursting shells, and thus broke the ladders and tumbled the men down from top to bottom, crushing still more underneath.

Yet more men were found ready to push on to the sanguinary scene. More ladders had indeed to be procured, which caused another great delay, but as soon as they arrived they were quickly hoisted, and the precaution was taken this time to fix them farther apart, so that if more beams were waiting to be rolled over, they might not take such a deadly sweep.

The second attempt was more successful, for the ramparts were gained and the French driven back and a single piece of ground being thus gained, a footing was soon established for many more, who succeeded in turning round some guns and firing them along the ramparts, soon sweeping the enemy off them.

Fresh reinforcements on both sides shortly arrived at this, for us, successful spot, but the garrison was soon forced back into the town. The ramparts were then scoured, the breaches cleared, and the *chevaux de frise* pulled down, and the main body of the

English entered the town. Some opposition had to be overcome in the streets, but that was soon cleared away, and the French escaped to Fort San Cristoval.

Our troops found the city illuminated to welcome them, but nevertheless then began all the horrors that generally attended a capture by assault —plunder, waste, destruction of property, drunkenness, and debauchery. I was myself exempt from all this, owing to my wounds, which kept me in camp at the time the town was taken; but though I was at least a mile off, I could distinctly hear the clamour of the rabble, as the guns and musketry had ceased, and next morning I hobbled as well as I could into the town with the help of the handle of a sergeant's pike chopped up so as to form a stick, and there sure enough I found a pretty state of affairs. Pipes of wine had been rolled into the streets and tapped by driving the heads in, for any one to drink of them who liked, and when the officers tried to keep order by throwing all of these over that they could, the men that were in a state of drunkenness lay down to drink out of the gutters, which were thus running with all sorts of liquors; doors were blown open all through the city, both upstairs and down, by placing muskets at the keyhole and so removing the locks. I myself saw that morning a naked priest launched into the street and flogged down it by some of our men who had a grudge against him for the treatment they had met at a convent, when staying in the town before. I happened to meet one of my company, and asked him how he was getting on, to which he replied that he was wounded in the arm, but that he had got hold of something that compensated for that a little, showing me a bag of about a hundred dollars that he had succeeded in obtaining, and saying that I should not want whilst he had got it.

But whilst all this debauchery was going on amongst some of our soldiers, I will give a word of credit to a great many of the more respectable, who were trying as much as lay in their power to stop the ferociousness of the same. That morning I met many about, who said they were sorry to think that the soldiers could not carry it on without going to such excesses as they did, respectable houses being ransacked from top to bottom, with no regard to the entreaties of the few inhabitants who remained within the walls. Things that could not be taken were often destroyed, and men were threatened if they did not produce their money, and the women sometimes the same. Comparatively few murders were, I believe, committed, but some no doubt occurred.

It was not till the drunken rabble had dropped into a sound slumber or had died in consequence of their excesses, that the unhappy city became at all composed, but in the morning some fresh troops were placed on guard, and a few gallows were erected, but not much used. Two or three officers had been killed in the act of keeping order, and I have been given to understand that some of the fifth division, having arrived after most places had been ransacked, plundered their drunken fellow-comrades, and it was likewise reported that a few were even murdered. Lord Wellington punished all offenders by stopping their grog for some time, but in these times such scenes as these were generally found to occur after a place had had to be so hardly fought for. No doubt in the present day, at least half a century later, more discipline is observed in similar circumstances, which must be owned as a great improvement.

This same morning the garrison surrendered. Before the assault it had numbered about five thousand, but we found that some twelve hundred of these had been slain, and now the rest were prisoners, while upwards of one hundred and fifty guns, eighty thousand shots, and a great quantity of muskets and ammunition were taken in the place. Ours was a much severer loss, for nearly five thousand of our men, including three or four hundred officers, were either killed or wounded. But it must be observed that with the circumstances under which our troops had to fight it was a wonder that they entered the town at all that night, every obstacle that a cunning enemy could devise being there to be overcome. Every kind of combustible deadly in its action was thrown amongst the men, placed in readiness along the ramparts were trees, stones, and beams; and the worst of all was the fearful *chevaux de frise;* in fact nothing had been wanting to discourage the men, who, however, pushed on, being as anxious as Lord Wellington himself to get into the town.

All being now over, thoughts of Pig Harding, George Bowden, and our engagement, ran in my head, and how it had all failed, poor Pig having received seven shots in his body, and George Bowden having had both thighs blown off. Both must have met with instant death, and I myself had four wounds and was disabled for some time from getting about. I resolved then that I would never make any more engagements under the same fearful circumstances. We missed poor Pig more than any man of the regiment, for he passed many an hour away pleasantly with his jokes, being a thoroughbred Irishman, and not only that, but he supplied us with many an extra piece of tommy by his roguish tricks.

CHAPTER 14

I Make Corporal

A day or two after these events, the wounded were all conveyed to hospital, some to Elvas and some to Estremoz. I was amongst the latter, as was likewise my comrade whom I mentioned as meeting me in the streets of Badajoz, as we were considered better able to stand the longer journey, the distance on from Elvas to Estremoz being about six leagues the other side from Badajoz.

On our arrival at hospital, we were allowed to take in no spirits or wine, which, as we had lately had so much of them, seemed to be more of a hardship to us than our wounds: but we were not long in working a system by which we were enabled to procure something to drink. The window of our ward looked out into one of the streets, on the opposite side of which was a wine shop, which for some time tormented us horribly: it was something like the fable of the fox and the grapes, sour because it was out of reach. The man of the house was often at his door on the look out, the natives there seeming to suffer from that general complaint as much as in our own country villages, where if there is anything fresh in the streets, perhaps only a strange man, or even one of the inhabitants in a new coat or hat, the whole place works itself into an uproar.

We soon devised a plan to gain our desired end. There was in the ward a tin kettle, holding nearly two gallons, and having procured a long string we put our money into this, and lowered it to the Portuguese, who soon getting used to our plan would put the money's value in the shape of wine into the kettle and again tie it to the string, so that we could hoist it up to the window again. After that we arranged for our ward to be pretty well supplied with grog too in the same way. Some suspicions being entertained by the doctor on the inflamed appearance of our wounds, he told us two or three times that he knew we had been drinking something we ought not, and blew the sergeant of the guard up for not being more strict in his search at the door, little dreaming how we had contrived another way to get this aggravator of our wounds in. But the appearance of our wounds did not stop us from lowering the kettle, which soon went down twice and sometimes three times a day, for the neighbouring wards got scent of the affair, and sent money to be lowered as well.

Thus I passed about six weeks before I recovered sufficiently to get out of the hospital; but many were in a much worse state than myself, some losing their arms, some their legs, and some even dying of their wounds. One of the slug shots, however, could never be extricated from my knee, having settled into the bone. I felt it for some time, but in the end it ceased to trouble me, the bone having probably grown over it.

I was let out of the hospital as a convalescent, and billeted in the place at a house occupied by a widow and her daughter, who were very kind to me during my stay there, which was for about a fortnight. Then I received intelligence that a hundred and fifty others were well enough to rejoin the army, so I asked the doctor if I might accompany them. He told me that my wounds were not yet sufficiently set for me to undertake the journey; but I was by this time sick of hospitals, physics, Estremoz, and the lot of it, and was mad to get back to my regiment, so I went to the captain, who was still lying wounded in the hospital, and asked him to speak to the doctor to let me go. The result was that next morning I again saw the doctor, who said I could go, but I must abide by the consequences myself, as he would not be answerable for my safety; so about three days after that our little group started on the way to the army, which had meanwhile moved northward from Badajoz to Salamanca, about two hundred miles distant, which we found rather a tedious march in our then condition.

I had not been many days at Salamanca before a fever broke out, which I caught very badly, and so was ordered back into hospital at Ciudad Rodrigo, along with a number of fellow troops who were troubled with a like malady with myself. On my arrival at the hospital, my hair was cut off by order of the doctor, and my head blistered, and I had not been there many hours before I became quite insensible, in which state I remained more or less for three months, which brought on great weakness. I received kind treatment, however, from the doctor and our attendants, and was allowed to eat anything my fancy craved, and amongst other things, without having to resort to any contrivance as at Estremoz, I could get wine. After being in hospital nearly two months longer, my strength had come back enough to allow me to be removed out of the town to a convent, the very one before mentioned which I had helped to storm when we were throwing up batteries for the assault of the town. There I found a number like myself who had lately recovered, and amongst them some of my own comrades of my own regiment, which made the time pass more lively than if we had been all strangers. By the time my strength was sufficiently recruited to again permit me to go on active service, November had again come round, so that from the time of receiving my wound at Badajoz, at least seven months had passed away before I was free from sickness and in a proper condition to again join my regiment.

The army, including my regiment, had been all this time actively employed at Salamanca, Madrid, and Burgos, and after going through many long marches and retreats, had again formed at Salamanca, up to which place the enemy had closely followed them. But owing to the season being too bad now to carry on the war, both sides felt more disposed to remain inactive for the remainder of 1812, so Lord Wellington determined on putting his army in cantonments; and in proceeding to carry out that design, for the enemy had now abandoned following up his retreat, he touched at Ciudad Rodrigo, which afforded a fine opportunity, which I willingly took, of rejoining my regiment

I found that our regiment had taken at the famous battle of

Salamanca a splendid drum-major's staff from the enemy, which was stated to be worth at least £50, and it must have come in very useful, for ours was terribly worn and knocked about, being very old, having been itself taken from the French in Holland, during the commandership of the Duke of York.

Soon after I rejoined, we crossed the Agueda into Portugal again, to take up our winter quarters in that country. Although it was not many leagues from Ciudad Rodrigo to where our cantonments were to be, yet that small march seemed to be almost going to knock me up, for my leg did not seem altogether strong enough to bear much marching, both of the slug shots having entered the sinew under the knee, and while we were engaged in this march it was kept constantly on the move. However, after we had settled down for about three weeks, I began to feel more like myself, and was therefore enabled to take my regular amount of duty.

But after we had been in cantonments some four or five weeks, I was on sentry one day, when to my great surprise, a comrade came to relieve me some time before my usual time had expired, which made me think something must be wrong: so, of course, wishing to know something of the matter before I felt disposed to leave guard, I asked the man what it was all about, and he told me that I had been made a corporal in the seventh company. I would at the time have much rather remained a private in my own company than be made a corporal and be transferred to the seventh; it was certainly better as far as pay went, for I received seventeen pence, whilst before I had received only thirteen pence per day; but I was far from feeling at home in this company, as I lost all my old companions; and not only that, but I then stood six feet one inch high, whilst not one man in that company stood more than five feet seven inches. I made my complaint to the captain, who promised that as soon as there was a vacancy, I should go back to my old company, and that cheered me up a little, but made me look with intense anxiety for the change back again.

Until it occurred, however, I had to change my abode, and live with four privates of the same seventh company in a private house, the landlady of which kept as nice a pig in her sty as I had ever seen in the Peninsula. Close by our quarters was the officers' mess-room, the sergeant of which had offered our landlady sixteen dollars for her pig; but the old woman would not take less than eighteen; so instead of giving that he offered the four men billeted with me the sixteen dollars to steal it for him, in return for the old lady's craftiness, as he had offered quite the fair value. The deed was done that very night, the pig being conveyed out of sight to the mess room; and in the morning, when the old lady had as usual warmed the pig's breakfast, she found to her surprise the sty empty.

She soon made a terrible noise over the affair, and immediately suspected the man who had offered to buy it; which soon got to his ears, and obliged him to make away with it for a time, for fear of being searched; so he got some of the men to heave it over a wall at the back of the mess-room. The four men who had stolen it soon got scent of this, and wishing to serve the sergeant out for his meanness, and likewise have some of the pig, they went, unbeknown of course to him, and cut off about a quarter of it, which they appropriated to our own use, and brought back to be cooked in the old woman's house; so that the sergeant had better have given the two more dollars, and come by the whole pig honestly after all.

Some difficulty was experienced by my fellow-lodgers in cooking their portion, as the landlady had generally before got their food ready; but this was at length accomplished in our own private room, with a kettle that we had borrowed from the old lady herself. I likewise had a taste of the poor woman's missing pig, which we found to be very good and acceptable. Fortunately, she never suspected us at all, but often talked to us during our stay there, of her sad loss; and indeed she was in general very kind to us, often going so far as to give us some dried chestnuts, of which she had an abundance, for a treat.

After about three months' stay in this place, during which time my captain to my great satisfaction found an opportunity of putting me back to my own company, we marched to other quarters about three leagues off, in a village which had been for the most part deserted, and there we were cantoned, chiefly in empty houses. Whilst we were here, a very interesting piece of excitement took place, in which one of the officers of our company, a lieutenant, was the chief actor. He was an Irishman, and being likewise a Catholic, had been in the habit whilst staying at our late quarters of visiting a Catholic chapel; and there he had seen and fallen in love with a Portuguese general's daughter. Correspondence and meetings had followed, unbeknown to the girl's parents, but owing to our shifting our cantonments, some difficulty had arisen in the way of their engagements, and so I suppose they thought it best to arrange one final one, or at any rate one of which the memory was to last some time. One night, therefore, he proceeded with two of our company to the lady's house, where all arrangements had been previously made for conveying her from her private window into her lover's arms, ready to elope with him.

These arrangements consisted of a ladder to be placed at a window, and the goods that she intended taking to be ready on the back of a horse, and were all carried out by two of the domestic men-servants who had been bribed, and who also undertook to keep a good look-out until the eloping party had got quite clear. But, as it proved, a worse set of people could not have been entrusted with the matter, for no sooner had they received their money, and the little company had set out from the house on their way to the officer's quarters, than the two foolish Portuguese servants immediately raised an alarm, and a party of six, including these very servants, was sent in pursuit

They soon overtook the travelling party, which was obliged to walk slowly owing to the horse laden with the goods, and the pursuers being armed with sticks, an altercation consequently took place, in which the Portuguese succeeded in capturing the horse and baggage, but the officer fought bravely for his spouse and was well backed up by his men, so that he succeeded in carrying her off at any rate. One of the Portuguese, however, lost two fingers in the affray, which was an unfortunate circumstance, and after things had come to this crisis, they left off their pursuit and went home contented in having captured the horse and baggage. The lieutenant then succeeded in getting the lady to the cantonments without any further molesting, and on the following morning he took her to a neighbouring chapel and married her.

But the matter was not to rest here; for next morning the old general wrote to our colonel on the subject, and said he intended to take proceedings against the lieutenant for stealing his daughter, as he called it. Our colonel informed the lieutenant that he was to consider himself a prisoner, as in such times as these he ought to be thinking of something else but marriage; but after a fortnight's consideration the general gave in, and made it all up with his new son-in-law, who was released and likewise had his wife's horse and baggage given back to him. In return for his good luck he treated the whole of his company to a pint of wine, which was drunk in toasts to the happy couple.

CHAPTER 15

Battle of Vittoria

We lay quite inactive in our cantonments until May, when preparations for the ensuing campaign commenced in good earnest; and about the middle of that month we left Portugal, bidding *adieu* to that kingdom for ever, for we now hoped that the enemy would very soon be compelled to quit the two shattered countries of the Peninsula, where we had done so much, and of late done it with such success. Much more yet, however, we found had to be accomplished before that hope could be fulfilled, as I am now about to relate to the best of my ability. We first commenced our march in a northerly direction, crossing the River Douro in Portugal; and after about a fortnight's procedure through almost insurmountable difficulties we arrived at Zamora, a town in Spain, situated not more than twenty miles from the Portuguese frontier on the north bank of the said river. The enemy had been occupying it lately, but had abandoned it on our approach, so from Zamora we followed them to a place called Valladolid, about seventy to eighty miles off, and thence to Vittoria, a still longer march of at least a hundred and sixty miles, during which some slight skirmishing took place between the retreating and pursuing armies.

On nearing Vittoria we came up with the main body of the French posted on some admirable heights, which they had made great use of to prepare for a stubborn resistance: they not only having the advantage of the heights, but we the attacking party having to cross a river below by means of only narrow bridges, which was a great impediment to our progress.

We arrived and encamped here on the 20th of June. On reconnoitring the enemy's strong position much doubt was entertained as to our success, our army being much fatigued after its tedious march and likewise being very short of provisions. This latter circumstance caused many to set off that night in search of something to eat; but the only thing I with several comrades could find was some broad beans, and those we had to gather for ourselves: we got a good many, but we were certainly not out for them more than an hour altogether, as nearly the whole of my party had to go on duty that night, and as it happened at the general's own quarters, which were in a house which, had been deserted by its inhabitants. We occupied a kind of outhouse adjoining, and having lit a fire in the centre and found a kettle belonging to the house, we set to work and cooked a quantity of wheat that we found stowed away there, and on that made a very good night's meal. I likewise preserved a quantity and put it into my knapsack for a favourite comrade who had been left in camp in charge of our beans; but when I returned I found I need not have done that, for he had had just as good a meal off the greater part of the beans as we had off the wheat.

Next morning orders came to fall in under arms ready to advance and attack the enemy's strong position. Our division, together with the Third and Seventh, was ordered to advance against the centre of their lines, so we had to bundle the remainder of our beans into our knapsacks, for to use my comrade's expression, "it went hard to have to leave any tommy behind in such times as these." Before we could get at the enemy we had to cross a narrow bridge, which gave us some trouble owing to the enemy's cannon, which played pretty sharply on us: and a shell pitching into one of our ammunition waggons, it immediately blew up, carrying with it two horses and the unfortunate driver. But once on the other side of the river and formed into line we were up and at them in spite of a murderous fire which they kept up from their cannon. We soon neared them, fired, and then charged, and succeeded in driving the centre over the hill. A column of their body still appeared on our right, and we immediately received orders to wheel in that direction; but the sight of us, together with the play of our artillery on them, was quite sufficient to make them follow their centre over the hill, whither we pursued them, but were unable to come up with them.

I came across a poor wounded Frenchman crying to us English not to leave him, as he was afraid of the bloodthirsty Spaniards: the poor fellow could not at most live more than two hours, as a cannon-ball had completely carried off both thighs. He entreated me to stay with him, but I only did so as long as I found it convenient: I saw, too, that he could not last long, and very little sympathy could be expected from me then; so I ransacked his pockets and knapsack, and found a piece of pork ready cooked and three or four pounds of bread, which I thought would be very acceptable. The poor fellow asked me to leave him a portion, so I cut off a piece of bread and meat and emptied the beans out of my haversack, which with the bread and meat I left by his side. I then asked him if he had any money, to which he replied no, but not feeling quite satisfied at that, I again went through his pockets. I found ten rounds of ball cartridge which I threw away, and likewise a clothes-brush and a roll of gold and silver lace, but those I would not give carriage to. However, I found his purse at last, which contained seven Spanish dollars and seven shillings, all of which I put into my pocket except one shilling, which I returned to the poor dying man, and continued on my way up the hill.

There I saw a French officer come out of a low copse close by, and instantly fired at him, but without doing him any mischief. He made his way up the hill as quickly as possible, using his sword as a walking-stick, but a German rifleman who had been on the look-out cut off his communication and succeeded in taking him prisoner. I did not take any further notice of him, therefore, but proceeded along with my company still in pursuit of the French, who were retreating in all directions in a very disorderly state.

We might have taken hundreds of them prisoners had it not been for our officers, who in their flurry had mistaken them for Spaniards; for Lord Wellington had previously ordered the Spaniards to wear a piece of white substance round their left arm to make some distinction between the French dress and theirs, which was very similar; but the French had got knowledge of this, and a great number of them, who were obliged in their hurried retreat and on account of the difficulties of the road to pass near our lines, had adopted the Spanish white band. Still we fired at them both with muskets and artillery; but when the officers perceived the white on their arms, without bestowing any more consideration as to whether they were the enemy or the Spaniards, they immediately stopped us from doing so. As soon as the French in passing observed this, they sunk into the valley and piled arms as if they were allies; and directly an opportunity afforded itself, they again took up their muskets and fired right into our lines, doing terrible mischief.

I never in all the days of the campaign saw men in such a rage as ours were with the officers. I really thought that some serious consequences would ensue, but as it was, all fortunately passed off as well as could be expected after such a mistake. For if this trick had before been observed, we might have taken the whole body prisoners by a direct movement of our right flank, as no other way lay open to their retreat without their encountering great difficulties; but the chance was now thrown away, and repairs could not be made of the damage done; many in our line having lost their irrecoverable lives, and others being more or less injured. We had only to make what consolation we could from beholding the almost express pace of the party as it retreated from where lay our comrades, either as groaning, wounded, or shattered corpses.

After their signal defeat at Vittoria, scarcely anything was left open to the French but to cross the Pyrenees into their own territory on the other side. Numberless quantities of warlike instruments were captured, such as cannons, muskets, cartridges, and all kinds of ammunition, besides supplies for the army, food, clothing, and the like, which were considering our need at the time of great benefit to the Allies.

I myself had my feet new rigged after this affair, and it was certainly not before I wanted a covering for them; there was certainly a part of the upper leathers of my old pair of boots left, but the chief part of the sole was my own natural one belonging to my foot. I had some little difficulty in procuring them, however, I happened to see a shoe-wagon that had been captured from the enemy and was being fast emptied by a number of our men, so I asked the captain to let me fall out, as my shoes wanted replenishing. He only answered, "No, not until the enemy is fairly away, and then you may do as you please;" so I had to disobey orders again, and on the next halt step off to the wagon to see what I could find. There were, however, such a number on the same errand that I began to despair of getting any boots, but at length I succeeded in getting into the wagon, and I hove out a hundred pairs or so to the mob, while I took up six or seven pairs for myself, or rather some likewise for some of my comrades, in hopes of making off with them quietly.

My hopes, however, were far from being fulfilled, for no sooner was I off the wagon, than I was completely smothered with parties that wanted and craved for boots equally with myself; so I had to let all my lot go, finding that I could not get clear, and got back into the wagon. Then I threw out another stock to the barefooted mob, and replenished my own lot, this time, however, only getting five pairs, and of these I did not succeed in getting off with more than three after all.

I made back to my company thinking to be unobserved, but in that I was again mistaken, for the captain himself seeing me called out, "You will disobey orders then, will you? and what are you going to do with all those shoes?" I told him I was going to put on a pair as soon as possible, to which he replied, "Very well, sir, mind you give the rest to your comrades;" which I did, as that had been my intention from the first; if not, I should not have troubled to get more than one pair, as on such marches as ours it was not likely that any man would care to carry a change in boots, or of anything else but food, which, though seldom denied to us, was more seldom obtained.

At Vittoria, too, Buonaparte's carriage was captured with some ladies in it The French army had retreated to Pampeluna, so Lord Wellington sent a sergeant and twelve men under a flag of truce to escort these ladies into the French camp at that place, in return for which Buonaparte behaved very well, for he gave the sergeant a doubloon and each of the men one-half of that sum, and had them escorted out of his lines by a French officer.

Our army meanwhile pursued the enemy until night put an end to our proceedings, when we encamped two or three miles west of Vittoria, there remaining two nights and one day busily engaged on the forage for ourselves. Happily thousands of sheep were found, that the enemy had been obliged to abandon on their retreat. I had been fortunate enough to get one and bring it into camp, and was proceeding to kill it by putting my bayonet through the neck, when Lieutenant Kelly of our company happening to pass, "Hullo, Lawrence," he said, "you seem a capital butcher." I said, "Would you like a piece of it?" "I certainly should very much," he answered, "for I am devilish hungry;" so I took out my knife and cut off one of the quarters just as it was, without even skinning it, and gave it to him, saying, "There, sir, you must skin it yourself." He thanked me and said, "Never mind the skin, I will manage that."

Not only myself, but several of my comrades had likewise managed to get a share of these sheep, so that night a general cooking ceremony commenced our first movement being to go round and gather all the odd sticks we could lay our hands upon, including gates, doors, chairs, tables, even some of the window-frames being knocked out of the many deserted houses and gathered together in one heap for this great purpose; and in a very short time both roast and boiled mutton were seen cutting about in all directions. Nor had we altogether forgotten our former experience of the beans which were growing plentifully at that time and place, and we found that night's meal as good a one as we had tasted for some weeks past. After it was over we lay down for the night—a body picket having previously been sent out to guard against any surprise from the enemy; but we lay very comfortable without being disturbed the whole night, and as our fires did not cease burning we kept very warm as well.

Next day was likewise chiefly spent by those off duty in

search of food, some returning with one or more of such articles as wheat flour, cabbages, turnips, carrots, and beans. A fellow-corporal of mine seeing this, and neither of us having been out, said, "Lawrence, I'll go and try my luck too, and if the drums should beat for orders, you go and get them for me, and then we can share the profits of my search." I consented, and he soon went, and was gone for at least two hours before he returned loaded with his findings, having taken his shirt off and tied the sleeves and collar up, and then filled his impromptu sack quite full. He had evidently carried his burden no small distance, for on his return the perspiration was running down as big as peas. "Tare an' 'ounds," poor Paddy said, for he was an Irishman, "I've got a fine lot of flour, but am as tired as a dog, and as hungry as a hunter."

"Well done, Burke," said I, for that was his name, "we will soon have a blow out of dough-boys and mutton."

I accordingly got a tin dish which I took from a Frenchman at Vittoria, and having filled it with our supposed flour, I poured some water on it, intending to make some balls of dough for the pot; when I suddenly found Paddy had been making a great mistake and that it was nothing more or less than lime that he had brought instead of flour. I said, "I'll be bothered if you haven't brought home lime for flour;" but Paddy would not believe it, saying it was the best white flour, till I told him to come and see it boiling and smoking in the pot, which quite confounded him, and taking up the remainder in his shirt he hove it out, saying, "Well I'm blessed, comrade, if I ain't off again, and I'll take good care not to come back again this time till I have some good flour."

He had been gone about an hour when he returned with at least half his shirt full, for he had got on the same scent as a great many who had been before him and were now fast returning already loaded. I then commenced making the dough-boys by mixing a little salt and water with the flour, and put them into a kettle swung over a fire on two sticks placed perpendicularly on each side with a cross-bar on the top, gipsy fashion, and by night our supper was hot and well done. As is perhaps well known, dough-boys cannot be very greasy without fat or suet of any kind, but they were quite passable in the hungry state we were then in, and as we had no bread, we used some more of the mutton to help them down. Our fires were then made up the same as the night before, and at the proper time we again retired to rest comfortably and were soon lost in a profound slumber.

CHAPTER 16
Advance to the Pyrenees

On the day after the adventure of the dough-boys we were again ordered to march, and advanced towards Pampeluna, but that town being garrisoned by the French, we passed it on our left, and proceeding for some distance further west, encamped near some hills with strong fortifications on their summit. There we lay a few days, and thence arrived on the heights of Villebar in the Pyrenees in the latter part of July, where we took up our position. Lord Wellington had extended his army in a line along the Pyrenees which must have exceeded thirty miles from the extreme left to the extreme right, and which would owing to the difficulties of the mountain barriers have made it very hard to combine in case of an attack in force by the enemy on any particular part of our line. Thus in warfare such as has now to be described we ran more risk than the French, who being able to form in their own country and drive their body on any part of our line, had a considerable advantage over us.

Our division, with a brigade of the Second and another division of the Spanish, occupied the extreme right, covering Pampeluna. Very shortly after our arrival the action commenced on our left; and meanwhile suspicions were entertained that Soult intended to attack, so as to reinforce and throw supplies into Pampeluna, which was being blockaded by the Allies and in danger of capitulating owing to shortness of provisions. Lord Wellington accordingly sent our division to a particular pass of the mountains in search of the said supplies, and after marching over hills, mountains, and valleys for at least thirty miles, we at length fell in with about three hundred carts laden with provisions and ammunition. They were guarded, however, by a strong body of the enemy, who soon attacked us; but they met with a strong reception, and after a severe altercation on both sides we succeeded in capturing the booty. Owing, however, to the difficulty of the country, and our not having proper means of transportation, we were obliged to set fire to the bread of which there was a great quantity, although it was the very substance of which we were so much in need. It went very much against our will, but that being the order it had to be attended to, not, however, before some of our men had stocked themselves with a portion that could reasonably be moved. Then having placed the amunition together and extended a long train so that at any time it might be easily blown up, we retired some distance and waited for the reappearance of the enemy, who, most likely thinking we had abandoned some of the carts, were not long before they came back in strong force; and on their nearing the fatal machine the train was fired and a great number of them were soon launched into the air. We retreated after that as quickly as possible to Pampeluna out of reach of the enemy, falling back that day at least twenty miles; a hard day's work indeed, but not thought much of in those times, when equally hard days were so often passed through, especially in a hasty retreat or on a well-fought battle-field.

We again encamped for nearly a week, during which time we amused ourselves in throwing up huts for officers' quarters, cooking-houses, and the like; and we had settled down so nicely that we had almost begun to think we were to be stationed there for at least six months. But on the very next Sunday we found that we were mistaken and that our hopes were to be disappointed. A square had been formed into which a parson entered to read prayers and preach, and a drum being placed for his books and a knapsack for him to kneel on, he had proceeded with the service for some little time, when all of a sudden up he jumped with his traps and made a bolt, before any one had hardly time to see the cause, amid the applause and laughter of the whole of the troops at his running, which was as fast as his legs could carry him, and looked then as if the poor man might be going on even till now. They used to say that the three scarcest things to be seen in an army were a dead parson, drum-major, or a woman: the explanation of this was to be found in the fact that they were none of them, often to be seen on a battle-field; and I think in this case our parson must have told and frightened all the others in the kingdom, for never after that did we have any service in the field.

But the cause of the sudden flight on the part of the parson proved not to be one entirely of enjoyment, for a large body of the enemy appearing, we likewise found ourselves running about pretty smartly and preparing for immediate action. The affair lasted hotly till dusk, our division losing some four or five hundred men. When night fell we were obliged to retreat still further towards Pampeluna, leaving the wounded, with the exception of two grenadiers who had been shot in the thighs, and whom we took turns to carry in two blankets, in the enemy's hands.

We had to get through a very thick wood of quite three or four miles in extent, which took us the whole night to accomplish; and in the morning when we were finally through, we lay down like so many loaded donkeys; still obliged, however, to remain in readiness, as we expected to be pursued. And soon enough we found we were, for we had not lain down very long before the enemy came up and charged us hotly, again forcing us to follow up our retreat, without even thinking this time of our two wounded burdens, who were left to the mercy of the enemy. In a few hours, however, we again joined the main army, or rather got into its line; and pleased enough we all were to get back.

We were then posted in a strong position on the heights of Villebar with the Spanish troops on our right. The French soon made their appearance and attacked the Spanish corps, who fired at them long before they came within bounds of shot, not having proper officers to guide them; those that ought to have been leading them on having instead placed themselves out of the way, leaving their men to do the dirty work; and of course these latter soon decamped too. Our regiment, however, was soon on the scene, and hastening in that direction, we managed to get there before the enemy had gained the summit of this important ridge. Orders had been issued by our officers not to fire till we could do good work; but this soon came to pass, for the French quickly sallied up and fired first, and we returned it in less than a minute.

I never saw a single volley do so much execution in all my campaigning days, almost every man of their two first ranks falling; and then we instantly charged and chased them down the mountain, doing still further and more fearful havoc. When we had done we returned to our old summit again, where the captain cheered and praised us for our gallantry, saying that he had never seen a braver set of men, and that he hoped we would always succeed in preserving our ground equally well. Our likewise brave enemy tried again two hours later to shift us and take possession of our ground; but they were again received as before and again sent down the hill. We were again praised by our commander, who said, "I think they have got enough of it by this time, and won't make a third attack in a hurry;" but we were mistaken, for four hours had not passed before they were up again with fresh reinforcements. Some of our men then seemed to despair, for I heard them even say to the officers who were so bravely leading us on, "We shall have to be off this time." "Never mind," replied the officers, "keep your ground if possible, and don't let yourselves be beaten;" which we did like bricks, for on their arrival and trying to outflank us, so that we were obliged to wheel round to the left, the right flank opened fire as they were close upon us, and instantly charged right into them with the bayonet, forcing them to retreat

They again fell up to support their other companies, who were attacking our other flank; but we reloaded and were then ready to meet them, again pouring another of our deadly volleys into their ranks and then going at them again with our bayonets like enraged bulldogs. The fight that ensued was most sanguinary, but we succeeded again in driving them down the mountain at last. I should think they must have numbered five to our one; in fact the whole of our fourth division was attacked, but all assisted equally bravely in retaining our position on the heights and earned great praise from our commanders. I do not myself think, however, that we could ever have routed so large a number of the French had it not been for our advantageous ground. Some Portuguese troops likewise behaved very well, but as for the Spaniards, I can safely affirm that after their first retreat I did not see any more of them again that day.

We encamped that night on the same ground that we had so well defended. Our captain, who was as nice a man as ever commanded in the Peninsula, always seeming to share everything with the men and bear the blunt as well as the smooth, and the losses as well as the profits, now said, "Come, my brave men; turn to and cook yourselves something to eat, for you have earned it well;" an order which we soon set about to obey. A quantity of rum had been sent up for us, so we were able to sit down tired as we were and enjoy ourselves as if nothing extraordinary had occurred that day. We then sent out a picket and prepared to take our rest for the night, the French not seeming inclined to sally up any more to engage us on those heights.

When the returns were called off the list, we found our killed and wounded amounted to seventy-four, but one more of our number was soon to be added to the sum total. A comrade of my own company went in search of sticks to liven up our fire: I told him to be careful and not get in sight of the enemy's picket, or they might have a pop at him, and he replied never fear, he would be careful; but the foolish fellow had been gone but a few minutes, when he was shot through the neck. Instead of keeping his own side of the hill, he had diverged on to the other close enough to be observed by one of the enemy's riflemen, who shot him as I have described. I happened to hear the shot, and found that it had been at him, so I went and dragged him back, pretty quickly as may be supposed, for I was. fearful lest I should be shot likewise myself. The poor fellow was not dead, but exclaimed, "Oh, corporal, I am a dead man!" When I had got him out of the enemy's reach and near our own lines, I took his stock from off his neck and he expired directly; so I had to leave him and rejoin our company with the news that another of us was gone, making seventy-five in all.

On the following morning I happened to observe an officer of the French army moving at some distance in front of our lines, having hanging from his pocket a fine watch-guard, which particularly took my attention and which I thought at the time would look very well on me; and being more daring than wise, I crawled towards him. with my musket loaded, and when near enough as I thought to him, I fired; but it did him no mischief and only made him take himself off at once. I nearly got into a scrape through it, however, for I was fired at myself in return, the bullet fortunately only taking the butt end off my musket. I turned to run off, and another shot hit the knapsack on my back, but I soon got out of reach of their shot again, luckily, as it happened, without any injury; but it must have been a near thing, for when I next opened my knapsack, I found the ball had gone through the leather and my thickly-folded blanket and had at last been stopped by the sole of a shoe, and was lying there as flat as a halfpenny and about the same size.

The same day we were joined by the Fifty-third regiment Lord Wellington having sent it on to relieve us in case of another attack from the enemy. They offered to occupy our heights, so that we might fall back to the rear, but our captain would not consent to that; "For," as he said, "my men have fought well to defend their position, and I think they will be strong enough to keep it." He proposed, however, that they should keep out an outlying picket, so that we could take our rest, which would be the best way of relieving us, and their commander readily agreed to do so.

Thus we passed two or three days, both armies remaining inactive. Then one day a French officer was seen coming up the mountain, having laid down his sword, so our captain sent a lieutenant who could talk good French to meet him and see what he wanted. He found that he wished to know if we would allow him to send for their wounded, so an agreement was entered into that we should take all their killed and wounded half-way down the mountain, and that they should meet us there with ours in return. This plan was soon carried out; and when we had buried our dead, the wounded were conveyed to hospitals appropriated to them at the nearest convenient place.

All was still quiet on the following morning, but later in the day the whole body of our line appeared in motion, and we were ordered in company with the Fifty-third regiment to attack the enemy's post near us, acting in conjunction with the other front of our line; and this being done, we soon drove them right off the mountains. The Portuguese troops in our division fought well in this action. We followed up the retreating French to a village situated in a valley of the Pyrenees, where they were delayed owing to having to cross a river. General Cole immediately ordered our regiment up to stop them if possible; so off we went in quick time to the river, and on their seeing they were so quickly pursued and that there was no hope of escaping, they threw down their arms and gave themselves up prisoners to the number of about seven hundred.

We took a gold-mounted sword from their commander, and a gold plate out of his cap with an eagle engraved on it, which were given to our captain by the regiment as a present, as he was a universal favourite for his behaviour to the men in general.

The prisoners were then sent to St. Jean de Luz to be put on board ship, and so conveyed to England.

CHAPTER 17
I am Promoted to Sergeant

We marched slowly on, following up the enemy as closely as possible, often even having them in sight: and both armies were sometimes encamped for a week at a time, and employed meanwhile in skirmishing with each other.

At one of these halts the enemy by some means or other got three pieces of cannon on to the top of a steep mountain, probably by men dragging them up with ropes, as it was impossible for horses to have done it; and on our entering the valley, Lord Wellington happening to be with us, a shot from one of these carried his cocked hat completely off. Our colonel remarked to him, "That was a near miss, my Lord;" to which he replied, "Yes, and I wish you would try to stop them, for they seem determined to annoy us." Our colonel immediately said he would send some of the grenadiers up for that purpose, so I, being a corporal, and right-hand man of the company, volunteered with a section to undertake the job. Six men were accordingly chosen besides myself; rather a small storming-party for the object in hand, as they numbered twenty-one artillerymen and an officer, according to my own counting.

I led my little band along the valley and approached the mountain whence they were tormenting us. The artillerymen kept up a fire at us from the cannon, which consisted of light six-pounders, but owing to our movement they could not get the elevation. We slowly scaled the hill zigzag fashion to baffle their aim, until we got so close that the cannon could not possibly touch us, owing to a slight mound on the hill. We were then within a hundred yards of them, and I took their number, and found at the same time that they had no firearms with them but the cannon, which were of not much use at close quarters for such a few men. I should say we lay there on the ground for at least ten minutes, contemplating which would be the best mode of attack, while they were anxiously watching for our reappearance.

At last when ready I said, "Now my men, examine your flints and priming, so that all things may go right." They did so, saying, "All right, corporal, we will follow you;" so I too sang out, "Now for a gold chain or a wooden leg!" and having told them what to do and to act together, we jumped up, and giving them a volley, we charged them before they had any time to take an aim at us, and succeeded in gaining the cannon and driving the men down the mountain to a body of their infantry that was stationed at the foot I immediately made a signal with my cap for our brigade to come up, for they were all ready and on the watch, but we found that the enemy's infantry was likewise on the move for our height Fortunately, our brigade was the first to arrive, and reinforced us on the mountain, and on seeing this the enemy decamped. By great luck not one of my men was injured, whilst our volley killed or badly wounded five of the artillerymen.

After the enemy's retreat, the colonel came up to me and said, "Well done, Lawrence; I did not think you were half so brave, but no man could have managed it better." He likewise praised my six fellow-stormers, and a short time afterwards Lord Wellington himself came up and asked me my name, and on my telling him, said, "I shall think of you another day."

These three cannon, which were composed of brass, were now the only ones we possessed, as owing to the difficult nature of our route our own had been obliged to be left behind; even the cavalry being of very little use in this mountain warfare. Soon after this daring feat of ours, the enemy again commenced their retreat, we still following close up to them; but after proceeding some two miles, we found they had again halted and were occupying another mountain; so we sank into the valley, and made ourselves as comfortable for the time as we could under the circumstances. We had no tents, and even if we had, we could not have pitched them so close to the enemy, so at night we curled ourselves well into our blankets and retired to rest on the ground.

Finding next morning that they apparently did not mean to renew their retreat without being made to do so, we tried the experiment; but that day we were defeated in our object, for again, like the fatal fox and grapes, we could very well look at them but could not get them down. We accordingly brought up by the mountain again that night, and those who were not amongst the number told off for picket, which was large as we were so near the enemy, again retired to rest in their blankets. But next morning, not feeling contented with their prolonged stay, or with our attack of the day before, which had only failed to move them, we again assailed them; this time with success, for we drove them from that mountain and pursued them till they again halted. We followed their example, and then we lay again for several days, getting good and undisturbed rest every night, and only having to send out a picket so as to guard against any surprise from the enemy, this duty, of course, falling equally on all in their turn.

I think it was about the third day that we were put into advancing order and were again led on to the attack. When we got within a few paces, we gave them our usual volley, and made our charges, which they did not long stand against before they again started on a slow retreat, we always keeping pretty close to their heels and being very often occupied in skirmishing with them.

I was engaged myself in one of these affairs that happened during a short stay that we made. A small body of us were out under a sergeant, an Irishman named Ryan, and observing a large force with some of the enemy lurking around the premises, we made towards it and drove these few off the place, after which four or five more came out of the house on our approach and decamped. We entered and found a pig there just killed; but the butchers had evidently not had time to open it, so we set about taking our turn to do so, but were not allowed time to finish the job, for we now perceived a large body of

French fast coming up, and we in our turn were obliged to retreat. Sharp enough work it was for us, too, for they had got within bounds of shot, and certainly did not fail to make use of it, following us up and firing at us across a meadow, which I can well remember was surrounded by a very thick thorn hedge, which delayed us very much, as we had to jump over it; and I not being much of a jumper myself, managed to find myself in the middle of it. It was a very prickly berth, and became more so when our sergeant, who had got clear himself, came to my assistance to pull me through. I got scratched all over, but that was not so bad as the thought of the bullets that were peppering through the hedge on all sides of me; however, I was extricated at last, though I left most of the back part of my uniform behind, and we proceeded at full speed on our way. We had not gone far, however, when our poor sergeant was shot down. He appeared quite dead, but I did not stop, for they kept on stoutly pursuing us until they began to be afraid of getting too close to our line, which by this time had made a forward move, both our army and the enemy likewise being still on the march, and we skirmishing with their rear.

At one time we came on about two hundred of their stragglers, and we fortunately numbering very strongly, were enabled to engage them and drive them back. Soon after this I had another very narrow escape. One of the enemy had lain in ambush in a thicket at the top of a mountain where I myself was straggling. I had no one near me at the time, and this fellow in the bush fired at me. The shot first took the ground and then bounded up against my brass breastplate, which was fixed on my cross-belt, and probably served on this occasion to save my life. The Frenchman, as soon as he had spent his shot, bolted; I had my own musket loaded at the time, but I did not think of firing, but proceeded after him with all my speed till I came up with him. I did not think I could run so fast. I have made Frenchmen run before, but it was generally after me. When he saw he was outdone he showed very poor pluck, for he immediately threw down his arms and gave himself up to me. If he had had any spirit he would not have done that so easily, though certainly I was loaded, while he was not, having, as I before said, exhausted his shot, owing to my plate, however, I am happy to say, without doing me the slightest injury.

I then began to strip him of his accoutrements and ransacked his knapsack, but I was sadly disappointed in finding nothing about him; so I took his musket and broke the stock, and left him, not feeling inclined to be troubled with a prisoner, or to hurt the man in unfair play. And I likewise felt quite pleased at my narrow escape, as those sort of things often served as topics of conversation during our night lounges when we were in pretty quiet quarters. The man himself seemed very grateful that I did not hurt him after his offence; and the more so when I returned him his not-fit-for-much kit in his knapsack, nothing of his, in fact, being damaged except his musket; and he walked away with an air of assurance, without appearing to be in any hurry or afraid of being overtaken by any other of our men.

I then went on in search of my comrades, who had by this time left the mountain for the neighbouring valley, and after running down the slope, I found them posted in a house situated at the bottom. They had been in search of provisions, but all they found was a cask of sweet cider, the French having evidently been there before us and the place having been ransacked of everything but this. We drank as much as we wanted and put the rest into our canteen, but we were greatly disappointed in not finding anything to eat, for we were dreadfully hungry and very short of provisions.

However, after we had refreshed ourselves with the cider, at which our officer helped us, he ordered us to be getting on, or rather led us on himself to a small village about half a mile off, which we knew was occupied by some French. We found that a river intervened between us and this village, with a bridge over it guarded by about two hundred of the enemy; and a long lane had likewise to be traversed before we got up to them, in passing through which several of our men were wounded either by some of the enemy lying in ambush or by stragglers. Still we did not take long altogether in arriving at the bridge, and when there, having our firelocks all ready, we opened fire and then charged; but our attack was in vain, for we were met and overpowered and obliged to retreat behind a large hill at a short distance from the bridge. In the course of this short action I saw the French officer's horse shot from under him, but whether he was injured himself I cannot say.

We rested a short time behind this hill, and came to a determination to make another attack on the bridge. This time we met with more success, for though we only effected it after a long and severe brush, we made them retreat, leaving the hard fought for but really insignificant bridge in our possession. We found nearly thirty of the enemy lying there killed and wounded, while we only lost about fifteen in all. But we did not delay over our captured bridge, for the blood of victory once in our veins, we pressed on for more and traced them down, continually firing as we passed through the village.

Unfortunately I sprained my foot here, which disabled me from following, and a Portuguese inhabitant having asked our officer to let one of our men stay in his house to guard it from plunder whilst we remained in or near the village, the officer said to me, "Corporal Lawrence, you may as well stay with the man as you are so lame, and it will do to give you a rest." The company was to go back to the house where the cider had been found, so I was rather glad of this occurrence, as I calculated I should get more attention paid me than if I had been with my comrades. I accordingly seated myself near the door of the man's house, and he soon brought me about a pint of wine with a piece of bread, for which I was very grateful, as I was very hungry and the wine proved to be much more to my taste than my previous ration of cider.

I had not been sitting there long, however, before I heard a heavy footstep descending the staircase of the house, and on looking up, found it belonged to a Frenchman who had been up there for the purpose of plunder, and was now coming away with a good-sized bundle of clean linen under his arm. When he saw me he immediately bolted out of a back door which led into a field. I made a desperate plunge at him with my bayonet, but owing to my bad foot I could not get near enough to him to hurt him; still I managed to stop his burden, for he had forced that against the bayonet to shield himself from it. As soon as I could extricate my musket, I hobbled as quickly as I could to the back door and sent a bullet after him; but he had got some distance away, and, I cannot say exactly whether I hit him; though I think it broke his arm, for I saw it drop immediately, and his motion became more slackened as he passed out of sight, which contented me as much as if I had killed him.

I then went back into the house and blew the Portuguese up for not keeping a better watch than to let a Frenchman find his way upstairs, as he might have killed us both. The Portuguese said he did not know how he got up there, neither did he very much care so long as he was gone now. I told him I thought he was a very easy-going customer, and pointed out that I had saved his linen for him, and his wife took it upstairs again as if nothing had happened, he likewise remarked that there was no fear of the Frenchman having taken any money, for he had none. He then gave me some more bread and wine, and when I had stopped two or three hours longer, during which time I drank the wine and stowed the bread into my haversack till I should feel more inclined to eat it, I left them, not feeling altogether safe there, as the enemy might very likely fall back. I returned over our well-deserved bridge to the cider-house, as we had named it after the barrel we had found there. On my arrival my comrades seemed to smell out my bread, and they came and hovered round me like bees while I divided it as well as I could, for I was not hungry myself, and it was soon devoured.

We only stayed about two or three hours longer at this house until the army came up, and we again joined our different regiments. We halted near this place for the night, and our butchers commenced work killing bullocks for our supply. I think scarcely a drop of blood was wasted, for even that was caught in our kettles and boiled and eaten, and was found to be very good. Each sergeant had to send in his return for the meat required for his company, at the rate of two pounds for each man; and when he had received it, the cooking immediately commenced.

This was the last cooking that my fellow-corporal Burke, whom I have referred to before, ever took part in. But before relating how that happened I may as well mention that the butchers were entitled as a sort of perquisite to the bullocks' heels, which they sometimes sold. Burke bought two of these at this place for fifteen pence, and began cooking them in a somewhat peculiar manner, being either too hungry or too impatient to cook them properly by boiling. What he did was to put them on the fire to fizzle just as they came from the butcher, not even cleaning them, or taking any of the hair off; and every now and then he would gnaw the portion off that he thought was done, in order to get the underdone part closer to the fire. In this way he finished both the hocks, and for a time seemed satisfied, evidently thinking he had had a good supper.

But he had not counted on his digestion, for having eaten so much on an empty stomach, and that too almost raw and mixed with a fair amount of soot, for the fire was not altogether clear, it was not long before he felt it begin to disagree with him, and he commenced to writhe about and was in fearful agonies all night. The doctor of the regiment was sent for, but he could do nothing for the man, and in the morning he was no better. We were then ordered to follow up the enemy, so that he had either to march on in this state or be left behind. He chose the former, so I got him along by helping him for about a mile, when he suddenly without saying a word to any one fell out of the ranks, lay down on a bank by the roadside, and expired in a few minutes. I was very much hurt at this, for he was one of my best comrades, but there was no help for it, and we had to leave him and march on.

We did not come in contact with the enemy at all that day, and encamped for the night, as we thought, but it afterwards proved to be for nearly a fortnight. Towards the end of that time, our captain, who was my best friend in the whole regiment, rejoined us, having been left behind owing to a slight wound which he had received while on the march three or four weeks previously, but of which he had now quite recovered. Our company was at that time very short of sergeants, for which I shall afterwards account, so he recommended my promotion to fill one of the vacancies to the colonel, who gave him a written order for the purpose, and I was put into the place of poor Ryan. I of course was very proud of my new title, and not only that, but I received one shilling and eleven pence pay per day, being an additional sixpence on what I had formerly.

CHAPTER 18

San Sebastian & Nivelle

Very shortly after my promotion we were ordered to St. Jean de Luz, where we received new clothes, and high time it was that we did so too, for our old ones were scarcely worth owning as rags and fearfully dirty, the red of them having turned almost to black. I ought to have received a sergeant's suit, but owing probably to the quartermaster's obstinacy I only got a private's, the same sort as I had had before. Here we likewise received a good supply of bread and rum, which seemed to us like a new and even a luxurious diet.

I may as well here give the details about the sergeants of our regiment. I was the only one in my company where there ought to have been six when I was promoted, so the whole duty fell heavily on me. The rest had been wounded at some time or other before, and then never pushed on much to get back to their regiment; many when recovered preferring to skulk in the hospitals in paltry situations such as doorkeepers or ward-masters, so getting a little extra pay, and then, as I shall again have occasion to show, being too ready to make their appearance when the war was over. Fortunately, however, they then met with no great encouragement. They had really plenty of opportunity to follow up the regiment if they had chosen, but I suppose they thought they were best off out of the smell of powder, and probably they were, but still that does not throw a very creditable light on them.

After we had received our clothes and provisions, we did not lie long at St Jean de Luz, but again started on our marches, cruising about in the Pyrenees. For some time nothing of any particular note occurred until we again fell in with the enemy, who were stationed in huts which they had erected in the various valleys. We attacked them, and some sharp work ensued, for they did not seem to like the idea of abandoning their houses, which were much more comfortable than the open winter air, but we at last drove them off and took possession of their habitations, which a part of our army occupied. As for our regiment itself, we marched up the side of a mountain and encamped there.

We again found ourselves very short of provisions there, and besides that the rain was falling in torrents all night. We had nothing over our heads at first to cover them, so we set to and gathered a quantity of grass, sticks, stubble, and like things, and made a kind of wall to keep off a little of the wind and beating rain, and then we tried to make up our fires with anything we could get together, but owing to the wetness of the substances, they were not very lively, and it was a long time before we could get them to burn at all.

Our captain asked me if I could boil him a piece of beef, so I told him I would try and see what I could do to make the best of the bad circumstances, and accordingly I and a corporal of my company at once set to work, first placing our hanger over the fire and then swinging the kettle on it with the beef. The beef nearly filled the kettle, and though it was pouring with rain, it was a very awkward place to get water, as there were no springs near and no tanks to catch the rain in; consequently we had only about a quart of water in the pot, which had all boiled away before the beef was done. However, the captain was impatient for his supper, so it was taken up to him as it was, the pot-cover serving as a dish and a wooden canteen as a plate. I put it before him with salt on the edge of the canteen, and I likewise got him a piece of bread, which by the time he had it was nicely soaked by the rain—indeed we had not a dry thread on us by this time. The next bother was for a fork: I had a knife myself, but had lost the fork, so I got a stick and sharpened it at one end and gave him that as a substitute, and was rewarded by his praising me for my good contrivance.

Colonel Thornton coming up meanwhile, he was invited by the captain to partake of some of the beef, and he gladly accepted, as he said he was very hungry; so another plate, knife, and fork were wanted. I borrowed my comrade the corporal's canteen and knife, and manufactured another fork like the former to serve for the colonel, and they both said the beef was very good, but not very well done, which it certainly was not, for though it went down sweet like most things in those times, the inside was certainly hardly warm.

The colonel sent me to the quartermaster for a canteen of rum, which was equivalent to three pints, for which purpose another canteen had to be borrowed, but when I returned to him with it he said, "That's right; now go and drink it." I took it off to my comrade, and we both sat down under our artificial wall close by our fire to try and enjoy ourselves as best the inclemency of the weather would allow us, keeping, however, near our officers' green-carpeted nature's dining-room, so that if we were wanted we could hear them call. But when they did so, which was in a short time, it was for us to clear away, with orders at the same time to keep the remainder of the beef for ourselves; so we removed our dinner traps, passing a good many remarks in a jocular spirit on our green pasture, wet cloth, and our scientific dishes, plates, knives, and forks, much to the amusement of the colonel and captain who were looking on, and then sat down to our own supper, which we very much needed. I remember remarking to my comrade that we had not done so badly over our cooking after all, but perhaps it was only the hunger that made us think so. After finishing our supper and drinking the greater part of our rum, which no doubt got to a certain extent into our heads and served to keep out the cold and wet and make us generally comfortable, we curled ourselves into our blankets and lay down on the wet ground to rest.

The rain descended in torrents all night and completely soaked us, but the morning broke out clear, and after we had disposed of the rest of our beef and rum, we joined all hands at work in wringing and shaking the water out of our blankets before putting them up into our knapsacks. We were obliged to do this while they were damp for fear of an attack from the enemy, it being a general rule to keep all in readiness, and, indeed, on this occasion it was not more than an hour after these preparations that the French assailed us. Not being willing to show fight, we retreated on that occasion, having nothing to attend to but ourselves and our kit, for we were without baggage and cannon. After a ten miles' journey or so we again halted expecting to be attacked again very soon, for which emergency we hastily prepared, needlessly, as it proved, however, for we eventually stopped here quietly for a month.

During this time that I have been speaking of the siege of San Sebastian had been going on, the town having up to this time been already attacked twice, but without success. Lord Wellington now ordered twenty men out of each regiment of our division to act in conjunction with the besiegers, and soon after they arrived, the order being given to attack, after about two hours' fighting they succeeded in capturing the town and driving the garrison into the castle, which was likewise obliged to surrender in about a week. Though there were many deaths occasioned in this siege, strange to say the whole twenty men of our regiment returned unhurt.

I remember during our stay here, our captain was fearfully troubled with the toothache. At last one night, after trying in vain to endure the pain, he came to me and said, "Oh, sergeant, I am still troubled with the pain! What can you advise me for it?" I recommended him just to take a pipe of my tobacco, for I knew that would be a good thing for him, but he never could bear tobacco, so that it wanted a good deal of persuasion to at last make him consent to prefer the remedy to the pain. As he had no pipe of his own, I supplied him with the implement and some tobacco, and he began to smoke. But he had not been at it long before he said, "Why, sergeant, this will never do! The place seems whirling round. Here, take the pipe, for I feel precious queer; but my tooth is much better, and after all you are not such a bad doctor." He gave me half a pint of rum, and for a long time I heard nothing more of his toothache.

We stayed here, as I said before, about a month, and then again moved on after our enemy, our cavalry, pontoon bridges, and artillery coming on by the most convenient passes of the mountains. While on the march we often had slight skirmishes with the enemy, but no regular pitched battle until we came to the Nivelle, where Soult had taken up a strong position. There our army halted in line, determined to attack and proceed if possible into France, as nothing more remained to be done in the Peninsula, Pampeluna having been obliged, owing to short-ness of provisions, to surrender on the last day of October.

The Third, Fourth, and Seventh divisions, under Marshal Be-resford and their respective generals, occupied the right centres of the line. We commenced the attack early on the 10th of No-vember on a village which was defended by two redoubts. One of these our division took under General Cole, driving the en-emy to some heights in the rear, where we again attacked them and drove them over the Nivelle.

After this we went into cantonments for a few weeks, but owing to the unsettled state of the French army who had at-tacked our left, and then, having failed, had proceeded against our right which was commanded by Sir Rowland Hill, Lord Wellington ordered the Sixth and our division to reinforce the right. We only arrived there, however, just in time to hear that the action was all over, the defeat of the enemy and their en-forced retreat still further into their own country having been accomplished without our assistance.

CHAPTER 19

Advance to Orthes

After remaining inactive for the most part during the rest of 1813 and until the February of the next year, we again made an attack on the French, who were lying near a village of which I do not remember the name, and drove them behind a river. There they took up a fresh position, but retained it only two or three days, again shifting and opening a way for us to proceed on our way to Orthes.

And so after nearly six years of deadly fighting, we had got clear out of Spain and Portugal and carried the war into our enemy's very kingdom. Portugal and Spain had long had to contain the deadly destroyers, but now the tide was changed, and it was the inhabitants of the south of France who were for a time to be subjected to the hateful inconveniences of war. They had little expected this turn in their fortunes Napoleon had even at one time had the ambitious idea of driving us out of the Peninsula, but he now found us forcing his own army into its own country he had at one time thought that he would subdue Europe, but had while labouring under that error been subdued himself.

And all this was very much to our gratification, for we had long been looking forward to this result, being entirely sick of Spain. As for those places which had become so famous through us, we could not help thinking and referring back to the many comrades we had left there in their cold graves. Since our regiment had left for Ireland on this expedition nine hundred strong, fifty-one hundred men had joined us from our depôt, but at the time of our march to Orthes we did not in spite of this number more than seven hundred. I do not mean to say that we lost all these in battle, though I can safely say we did the greater part, either killed or badly wounded: but of course many must be reckoned who fell by disease, or as some did from their own drunkenness or gluttony, assisted by the inclemency of the climate, nor must those skulkers, of whom there must have been so many through the whole campaign, be forgotten.

Lord Wellington had watched with hatred the many excesses committed by the enemy on the Portuguese and Spanish inhabitants during the late campaign, and had determined, now he had carried the war into France, to set them for the future a better example; and accordingly he issued a proclamation that no plundering was to be carried on, on pain of death, which was much to the credit of our noble commander.

We arrived in France at a wrong time of the year to see its beauties, but from what I could then judge it abounded in elegancies and varieties of taste, such as vineyards, oranges, pomegranates, figs, and olive-trees to any extent, not altogether unlike the productions of Spain.

On nearing Orthes, we found the French had taken up a very strong position on a range of fine heights stretching from Orthes to St Boes, and we were ordered in conjunction with the Seventh division to cross a river and attack the latter place, which had one of the heights occupied by the enemy at. the back of it, giving them a commanding view of the place. Some delay was occasioned at the river, for there being no bridge, a pontoon was obliged to be thrown across; but this being accomplished, our divisions were soon over it, and being joined by a brigade of cavalry and artillery, we formed line and marched on St. Boes. The village was stoutly defended by the enemy, who on our nearing them fired briskly at us, for a long time standing their ground and trying hard to retain their charge, but they soon found they had sharp taskmasters to deal with, for our troops of the Fourth division under General Cole poured in on them like lions, and forced them after a violent resistance to start out of the place and take refuge on their strong heights.

We followed them up, but found that there they were for a

long time more than a match for us, as they had such an advantage in the ground. We rushed up the formidable heights, but were again and again driven back by the fearful play of the enemy's artillery, the position being only accessible in a few places, and those so narrow that only a small body could move on them at once. But even with these disadvantages and the enemy's cannon playing on them our men, after receiving fresh and strong reinforcements, carried the heights; and not only this, but the whole of the army having been similarly engaged on the right, had meanwhile succeeded in driving the enemy from their lines there, capturing a great number of prisoners in their retreat, the cavalry pursuing them closely; and some field-pieces were likewise taken.

The enemy then fell back on the River Adour, the allied army soon following and engaging them in slight attacks in various parts of the line, till at last the French again took up a position on the heights near the town of Tarbes, on the said river; but they did not stay long there, being soon driven away by the Allies and retreating towards St Gaudens. Thence they were again driven with great loss to themselves and a very trifling one to the Allies, this time to Toulouse on the Garonne, where they stood on the defensive on some more heights on the right bank of the river with every assailable part strongly fortified.

Some difficulty was met with in our march, owing to the chief of the bridges being destroyed and having to be replaced by pontoons, and those that were not destroyed being strongly fortified. One of these was guarded by some French cavalry, whom we annoyed very considerably by our fire as we approached them, having in case of their making an attack on us a fine artificial ditch to fall back into where it was next to impossible that they could get at us, our fire was made more daring by our knowing there was a body of hussars waiting out of their sight, ready to fall on them if they moved on us. We soon enticed out a body of about three hundred, who crossed the bridge under our retreating and destructive fire, and on their near approach we fell into our ditch, while at the same time our cavalry came up, and some close shaving ensued, a large quantity of spare heads, arms, legs, as well as many horses being soon strewn about the ground.

But this was not the worst part of our day's work, for after they had been tumbled back over the bridge, our division came up and we followed them right up towards their heights, keeping Toulouse some distance to our right. Before we reached the heights, however, we had to attack and carry a small village they were occupying. This was the commencement of the action of that bloody day which cost the armies on both sides numbers of their best men. It was fought on the Easter Sunday of 1814.

From the village we proceeded over some difficult ground to attack their right under a brisk fire from their artillery, so brisk, indeed, that one of General Cole's orderlies had his horse shot under him; and then we formed line and dashed up the hill, which was defended by some thousands of the French, nearly half of whom were cavalry We soon returned their fire, which at that time was a perfect storm of grape and canister, and directly we got near we charged them, but in vain, as owing to the sudden appearance of some of their cavalry we had to halt and form square: and indeed we must have been routed altogether by their combined infantry and cavalry, had not our Rocket Brigade stepped forward and played fearful havoc among their cavalry, driving them back. I had never before seen this rocket charge and have never either since, by all appearance it was most successful in this case, for it soon turned them to the right-about, and made them retreat.

The Spaniards were chiefly engaged on our right, and I never saw them fight better, for they seemed on this occasion as determined as the British and indeed of the two they suffered most, as the French, knowing them to be cowards, thought they would be certain of some success in that quarter, but they stood their ground well, only a few of their number getting into confusion.

When once we had gained this advantage and taken a part of their heights, our artillery joined us, and their play together with our action soon made the French fall back on their works at Toulouse, whilst we remained on our newly won height overlooking Toulouse and there encamped. I remember well the loss of a man in my company in this action, who had entered the army during the war for a period of seven years at first, and this period having expired for some time, he was mad to be out of these constant scenes of bloodshed and conflicts, but owing to the continuation of the war he had not been allowed to depart. He was not the only one in this plight, for there were thousands of others like him in the army, and several in my own company alone. Sixteen guineas had been offered to each for their services for life, and many had accepted, while many had refused, and of course amongst the latter was the man of whom I am speaking. His name was William Marsh, and he was a native of Bath in Somerset. He was by trade a tailor, and earned many a shilling at his trade in the army from various of his comrades who employed him. As I said, the poor man was sick of war, and before entering this very action had been wishing he could have both his legs shot off, so that he might be out of the affair altogether; little expecting that it might really be the case, or nearly as bad, for he had not been in action long before his wish was accomplished, as he was shot through the calves of both his legs by a musket-ball which took him sideways and pierced right through. Poor Marsh did begin to sing out most heartily, and I couldn't help saying, "Hullo there, Marsh, you are satisfied now your wish is fulfilled, I hope." He begged and prayed me to move him out of the thick of the fight, so I dragged him under a bank and there left him, and from that time till now I never saw or heard anything more of him. He was far, however, from being mortally wounded, though perhaps from neglect it may have turned to something fatal.

Another of our comrades in the front of our line had his foot completely smashed by a cannon-ball pitching right on to it, yet he managed to hobble to the rear in that state on his heel. I felt quite hurt for this poor fellow, who was a brave soldier, and seemed to be enduring great agonies.

Night having drawn in, all firing ceased, and the men set to examine the ground they had gained, chiefly to find firewood. I happened to be about when I came across a Frenchman who had been badly wounded and had crawled under a bank I went up to him and asked him if I could do anything for him. He had been shot in the stomach, and when he asked for water and I gave him some out of my canteen, which was nearly full, of which he drank heartily, in a very short .time it only fell out again through his wound. But the most astonishing thing was that he pointed me out his father's house, which was as far as I could judge about half a mile off, and said that he had not seen his parents for six years, for since he had come back to this place, he had not been able to fall out to go and see them. He begged me to take him so that he might die there in the presence of his parents, but I told him I could not do that, as there were a quantity of French there. However, I got an old blanket and wrapped it round him, making him as comfortable as I could under the circumstances, and seemingly much better resigned to his fearful fate, and then I left him and returned to my own place of repose, and after eating my supper and drinking my allowance of grog, I wrapped my own blanket round me, lay down, and was soon unconscious in sleep. I woke early in the morning, and having nothing particular to do, I crept out of my blanket and put all things straight; and then, more out of curiosity than from any other motive, proceeded to the poor Frenchman to ascertain if he was yet living; but his death must have taken place some hours before, as he was quite cold and stiff.

The loss of the Allies in this conflict was over four thousand in killed and wounded, more than two thousand being of the British, whilst that of the enemy was upwards of three thousand. But then there must be considered the advantageous ground they fought on, and the fearful havoc they made in our ranks before we were able to return a shot.

Lord Wellington now finding that Toulouse would not surrender, ordered fortifications to be thrown up for the reduction of that place, but they proved to be unneeded, for in the dead of the night the French disappeared from the place and retreated in a south-easterly direction towards Villefranche. We were soon following them up, and part of our army had slight skirmishes with them, but we never again saw their main body in that part of their country, for a day or two after our move from Toulouse the news came of Buonaparte's overthrow and the proclamation of peace, Buonaparte himself having been sent to the island of Elba. This was indeed good news for most of our troops certainly for the young officers it took away many chances of promotion, though it made death less likely as well, but ambition sometimes leads a man a long way out of his course, and very often adds tenfold to his sorrow. After the arrival of this welcome news, we encamped for three or four days longer to give our commander time to form his next plans. We were then ordered to Bordeaux to ship for our isles, the Spaniards and Portuguese being sent to their own country.

CHAPTER 20

The End of the War

Things now seemed to assume an entirely different aspect, indeed to take a new birth altogether. All were in a most joyous state, and none more so than the Spaniards, who were always only too ready to give up fighting. The Portuguese had always shown themselves the better race in the field of action, but they likewise now enjoyed the thought of returning to their own country, although it had been so pillaged. I had many a long conversation with stragglers of both these nations before we started on our long march, and so I had an opportunity of studying their thoughts on the subject.

We did not seem to be in any hurry to quit the country before everything was thoroughly arranged, and having no enemy pushing on our rear, we were often billeted at towns and villages longer than we need have been, which caused our march to take more time to accomplish, but made it much more comfortable. We were generally billeted on the inhabitants during our halts, the best billets being of course chosen for the officers, then for the sergeants, and then for the corporals and privates, the numbers being suited to the accommodation of the places, but I very seldom had more than one with me besides myself.

The inhabitants could not have behaved better to us if they had been our own countrymen; and I well remember how at the last stage where we put up before coming to Bordeaux two of us, myself and a private of the same company, were billeted at quite a gentleman's house, the owners of which were unusually kind to us. We found we had completely jumped into clover, and fortunately it happened to be Saturday night, so that our halt was till Monday morning; not that Sunday in those times had been used to make much difference to us, for two of our bloodiest conflicts had happened on that day, but in this case, our haste not being urgent, it gave us a kind of sweet repose.

As soon as we arrived at our house we were shown into our room, which was a very nice one and beautifully furnished; and when we had taken off our accoutrements, we went downstairs to a sort of bath-room, where we had a good wash in tubs of water that were placed in readiness for us. Then the gentleman had some clean stockings brought up to us, and when we had made ourselves comfortable he sent up to our room a loaf of bread and a large bottle of wine holding about three pints, which we found most acceptable; and it not being long before the family's dinner was ready, our hostess would insist on our dining with them. For my own part, not being used to such pomp, and never having before even seen it, being more accustomed to the kind of dinners and suppers in which I have described our own colonel and captain as taking part, I would sooner have crept out of the invitation, but being pressed we consented, and having been shown into the dining-room, we sat down to an excellent repast with nobody else but the lady and gentleman.

The table was laid out most gorgeously with glittering silver, which came very awkward to our clumsy hands, as we had been more accustomed to using our fingers for some years; to set off which gorgeousness our waiter, who was evidently the family footman, wore an out-of-the-way fine and ugly dress, with his hair plastered up with white powder, of which I had such an aversion during the first part of my stay in the army. A most palatable dinner was served of which I freely partook, though I had very little idea of what it consisted, and some good wine was likewise often handed round with which our glasses were constantly kept filled.

After dinner was over, the white-headed gentleman entered with coffee, a fashion which then surprised us very much; but nevertheless, more out of compliment than because we needed it, we took a cup each with some sugar-candy which was also handed round to sweeten it. When that was finished, just to keep us still going, the gentleman asked us if we smoked, and on our saying we both did, the bell was rung, and the footman entering with tobacco, we took a pipe with the gentleman, the lady having previously retired into the drawing-room. Then getting more used to the distinguished style, and the wine no doubt having made us more chatty, we for a time thoroughly enjoyed ourselves with our pipes, and began to feel new men with all our grandeur.

We were next invited to partake of tea in the drawing-room, but being very tired, we begged to be excused; and this being granted, the bed-candles being rung for, and having wished him good-night, we went to our room and there had a hearty laugh over the evening's business; though we had not been able to understand half what the gentleman had said, not being used to the French so well as to the Spanish language. We retired to rest in a fine feather bed, which being a luxury we had not seen for years, was consequently too soft for our hard bones, and we found we could not sleep owing to the change. My comrade soon jumped out of bed, saying, "I'll be bothered, sergeant, I can't sleep here!" "No," said I, "no more can I;" so we prepared our usual bed by wrapping ourselves into a blanket, and then with a knapsack as a pillow we lay on the floor and soon sank into a profound slumber.

Late in the morning, for we had overslept ourselves, the servant knocked at the door and said breakfast was waiting; and in a very short time the master himself came up and knocked, and on our calling to him to come in he opened the door, and looking in, found we had been sleeping on the floor. On his wanting to know if there were fleas in the bed, or what was the cause of our lying on the floor, we made him understand as well as we could, but it must have been very imperfectly at the best. He then went down again, and we soon following him, found an excellent breakfast ready, of which we made a first-rate meal, and after they had left us, for they had finished long before us, my comrade and I agreed that we had fallen on luck now, and no mistake.

Very soon after we had finished our breakfast, the servant entered to conduct us to the drawing-room, which was splendidly furnished, though for my own part I would rather have been down in the kitchen. We went in, however, and our hostess took down a book describing the French and English languages, so that they might under stand some of our words better, and again asked us the reason why we did not sleep on our bed. I told her we had not slept on a feather bed for six years, and answered her other questions, giving her a slight description of the trials of a soldier in the time of war. She was very much touched, and could not forbear from crying, more especially when I added that two privates were to be whipped that very morning for having got drunk over-night and making a disturbance in the town, to serve as an example to the regiment. They had been tried by court-martial and sentenced to a hundred lashes, to be administered in the town and witnessed by the inhabitants.

Although it was Sunday, the drums beat for the regiment to assemble, and the men were brought into our square; and their sentence having been read in the presence of all, the first man was led to the halberds, and the drummers got ready to begin. But five or six gentlemen of the town made their way into our square and begged the colonel so hard to let them off, as that was the general wish of the inhabitants, that at last he dismissed the victims with a reprimand. The two then thanked the colonel, but he told them not to do so, for had it not been for the timely interference of the gentlemen, he would have given them every lash. All were then ordered to disperse, and I returned to my excellent quarters, where we again received for the rest of the day no end of kindnesses in the way of luxurious meals, luncheons, dinner, and coffee, together with plenty of wine, and before we went to bed, brandy was introduced as a finish and having taken a hot glass of that with water, we retired and slept in a similar way to the night before.

On the following morning we had to assemble by seven o'clock, so no time was allowed us for breakfast; but our host had ordered our canteens to be filled with their best wine, and a parcel of sandwiches to be made up for each of us. We shook hands with the gentleman, duly thanking him for his kindness, and, rejoining our regiment, were soon on the march again for Bordeaux, which being not more than a day's march distant we reached the same night. We encamped at a place two miles off the city on the banks of the River Garonne, to which even large ships were able to ascend. Here we lay for five or six weeks, during which time the inhabitants made many excursions from the city especially on Sundays, to inspect our army, swarms of costermongers likewise visiting us every day with wine, spirits, bread, meat, fish, and fruit of every description for sale. Every Sunday afternoon the bands of all the regiments played, while the French amused themselves with dancing, many of them, both male and female, on stilts, which entertained us more than anything, and besides this there were all kinds of other jollities in which our soldiers freely joined.

And now I will take the opportunity of saying a few more words as regards the skulkers. As soon as the peace was declared no less than seven sergeants of my own company alone had either at this place or on the march thither made their appearance from the snug dens where they had been lying, most of whom had been occupying themselves with some trivial employment in the pay of the Spaniards or Portuguese, but had now at this crisis abandoned whatever they had been doing, for fear of being left in the country, or perhaps because they thought that they might still come in for a share of the praise and pay. Before they appeared I was the only sergeant in our company, while if the proper number had been there, there would have been six. I do not mean to say that there had been no cause at first for their staying behind, for there were some laid up like myself at Elvas and Estremoz, but it was their duty to follow up the regiment when they were able, as I had done myself.

The captain of my company, who had been like myself through the whole campaign excepting when actually in hospital, pretended not to know them when he saw them, and asked them, "Where on earth do you come from? you certainly don't belong to my company, by your appearance." He then called me to say if I knew them. I remarked, "They seem to have been in luck's way about their clothes, at any rate;" and so they did, for whilst ours were as ragged as sheep and as black as rooks, theirs were as red and new as if they had never been on, and their shoes were to match, whilst ours were completely worn out by our continual marches, the captain's being quite as bad as any private's.

We found that two of these men had left the regiment for hospital on our retreat from Talavera, and had never shown themselves since, the others having been away in like manner for rather shorter periods. Now the whole had returned we were overstocked with sergeants, having two more than our complement, so our captain sent the two who had been longest absent to the colonel with a written request that they should be transferred somewhere else, the other five he allowed to remain, but only for as short a time as possible till he could get rid of them also, as he told them his company should not be disgraced by them longer than he could help. He likewise told them that many of his privates deserved the stripes more than they did; and indeed it was not long before he got them transferred, and their places filled up by some of the braver heroes from among such of the privates as had at all distinguished themselves in any conflict.

CHAPTER 21

To America & Back

After remaining at Bordeaux for five or six weeks the army embarked on board ships bound for various parts of the British Isles. Our regiment was again despatched to Ireland, most of us being Irish. We were conveyed thither by the *Sultan,* a fine man-of-war with seventy-four guns. We had a very good passage, and amused ourselves very much with the sailors on board, who on their part had many a good laugh at our general ragged appearance. We landed in Ireland at Monkstown, near Cork, and marched thence to Fermoy, whence after lying two three days in the barracks there, we proceeded to Athlone in West Meath, where we were stationed for about two months.

The regiment had never been settled with during the whole of our Peninsular trip of six years, though money had been advanced to us at various places, so now while we were waiting at this place the accounts were made up, and some of our sergeants found they had as much as 50*l.* or 60*l.* to receive. My own lot amounted to 40*l.* I being one of the younger sergeants. When our pay had been given us a week's furlough was granted to the whole regiment, and no doubt most of the money melted away in that period—at least, I know mine did, for not having been in the British Isles for so long, we were all resolved to have a spree. I never went away from Athlone, however, the whole time, but slept in barracks every night, though there was no duty to be done as the militia were ordered out for that. I knew that it would be useless to cross the Channel in that short time to see my parents, though I should have liked to have done so, but I did not altogether forget them, and wrote to them to ease their minds about my whereabouts; as I had written to them during my stay in the Peninsula, and I thought they might have been anxious about my safety when they heard or read about the scenes that were taking place there, as parents naturally are about their children, be they ever so rackety.

But we were not allowed to stay here even in peace long, for at the end of the two months we were again ordered on foreign service, and marched to a place called Mallow in Cork, whence, having been joined there by our second battalion, and having had all the men fit for service drafted out of that into ours, we proceeded to Cork itself. This was a fine place for our captain to get rid of the remaining skulkers, and he left them behind, much to their annoyance, in the second battalion.

From Cork we proceeded to the Cove to embark, after a stay in Ireland now of about three months altogether, and when all was in readiness on board the ships, we set sail for the West In-dies. It can be better imagined than I can describe in what sort of spirit we began this other war, scarcely having slipped out of one field before we were launched into another; but as they were the usual thing on our embarkations, the same scenes that took place at Portsmouth will serve to picture those at Cork: they did not tend to enliven us much, but they were soon forgotten when we got to work talking over and telling our new comrades the many tales of the Peninsula.

After launching out of Cork Harbour, however, a terrible gale blew up, which obliged us to put into Bantry Bay for a time. One of our ships was lost on the rocks, but fortunately all on board were saved. They had lost all their accoutrements, however, so they were taken on board various ships, and as soon as we got fairer weather we returned to the Cove to await a fresh supply, which was at least three weeks in coming. Then we again set sail, amusing ourselves on the voyage as we best could; and having good weather, we arrived as soon as could be expected at Barbadoes, and anchored there for a short time.

One of the captains of my regiment, who had probably seen enough of war to satisfy him, had before our start sold his commission to a younger officer who gave him 1200*l.* for it; but, singular to say, the very first night of this our anchorage this poor young man went to sleep on shore, and, catching a fever, was brought on board and a few hours afterwards was a lifeless corpse. Owing to the infectiousness of his disease, he had to be immediately sewn up with two of our large shot in a blanket, and the funeral service being read by an officer as there was no minister on board, he was put into the sea. From Barbadoes we sailed to Jamaica, and anchored off Port Royal.

A singular circumstance occurred during our stay there: a girl was discovered who had been concealed on board at Cork by some of the sailors in a bundle of straw unbeknown to the captain of the ship. This being the best place for shipping her back to England, she was obliged to leave her accomplices at once, and I being sergeant of the watch was called to take her on shore to Port Royal with two privates. We took her to a kind of public-house, where, although it was two o'clock in the morning, the people were still amusing themselves in dancing to some rough music of their own, the whole of them being blacks.

We asked for the landlord, and on his soon making his appearance from among the company, as black as a crow and still steaming with the dance, I inquired if the girl could have a bed there for the night. He said, "Yes, for a dollar." I thought that was a stiffish price for a night considering it was two o'clock in the morning, but I paid him the sum and left the poor unfortunate girl there while we returned to our ships. I was very sorry for her, as she seemed nearly broken-hearted, but I could do no more for her under the circumstances, and I hope she got safe back to England after all.

After about a week had elapsed a gun-brig arrived to convey us to North America, England being then at war with the Americans, and we went on in her to the mouth of the River Mississippi. There we disembarked into barges holding about a hundred troops each, and having been towed up by other small sailing and rowing boats to Orleans, were put on shore near that place, our body consisting of five English and two black regiments, with a battalion of marines.

137

We marched on the same day and encamped about two miles from the city. Skirmishing was kept up with this our new enemy during the night, but without any great casualty happening. On the following morning, however, we advanced in a body to attack a battery that had been constructed near the city, chiefly out of barrels of brown sugar. We were at first warmly received with the cannon and musketry planted there, but they soon got tired of our Peninsular medicines: I suppose the pills disagreed with them, for they were very quickly obliged to retire into the city and no more fighting ensued; and some terms having been hinted at, when the black regiments had eaten a quantity of the fortifications, which they seemed to be very fond of, and we had put some into our haversacks as likely to be useful to sweeten our cocoa, we returned to our boats, and dropping down the river to a piece of land called Dolphin Isle, there encamped again.

The island was uninhabited, except that there were plenty of alligators, racoons, and oysters there; but we had plenty of provisions, that is, in the shape of meat and flour, though no bread, which inconvenience was from the want of ovens. We soon set to work, however, to construct one by burning a quantity of oyster-shells for lime, and having mixed that with sand and water we made some very good cement; after which we got a lot of iron hoops from the vessels, with which we formed the arch, and so we put one oven together; and I much doubt if it did not bake as well as any English one, considering the style of dough that we had. After it had been found to answer so well, at least twenty more were constructed on the once desolate but now busy little isle. We were constantly on the coast in search of oysters, of which there was an abundance; and some of the more industrious of us even collected them for sale among the troops who either preferred buying them to taking the trouble of collecting them for themselves, or else were unable to go on the sands on account of being on duty. They were sold very cheap, however; I have known half a bushel go for one dollar, which was certainly not much for the trouble of getting them.

During our stay here a playhouse was likewise erected, and

some of the more clever among the officers and men amused the troops in that way. The scenery was rather rude, to be sure; but with these and various other games and freaks the three months that we lay there passed off very pleasantly The poor blacks, however, suffered dreadfully from the cold, it being then winter, and they had to be sent back to their own country long before we left.

Our chief reason for lying there so long was to see all settled and to wait for orders before we proceeded back to England. When the order did come, joy was in every mouth, for this was indeed a short campaign compared with our Peninsular affairs, and it may be supposed we were by no means sorry for that. We embarked on board the same ships, and again tacked to the West Indies to get provisions at one of the Spanish islands, where we took on board live cattle and water, and as food for the former a kind of cabbage, which on account of their size were called cabbage-trees.

Thence we proceeded on our route to Portsmouth, and had a very pleasant voyage with fair weather prevailing; but when near England we fell in with an English frigate, which informed us that Napoleon Buonaparte had left the island of Elba with a small force and had landed in France to collect more troops. This was indeed a disappointment to me, for I felt sure that if he again intended disturbing Europe, we should have to be on the scene again. But in another way it caused no small amount of stir on board, for the young officers, who were looking ravenously forward to promotion, were so rejoiced at the news that they treated all the men to an extra glass of grog, to make everybody as lively as themselves.

Nothing else of any particular note occurred on our voyage, and having arrived near Portsmouth a signal was raised, and we fell in on the quarantine ground, hoisting a yellow flag for a doctor to inspect us on board. When he came he found all on board our ship to be in very good condition, which was reported to the general, and the very next morning he signalled to us to weigh anchor and proceed to Flanders, so without setting foot on English ground we again went on our way to meet our common enemy This time, however, he was not in his old quarters, but in the north of France, where he had collected more than a hundred thousand troops.

I left Portsmouth this time with a good deal lighter heart than I had last, being now more used to war and hardships than to peace and plenty, though perhaps I would rather have landed than proceed on this errand; and, indeed, there were many of us who had left wife and children at home who went off with a very sad heart

Our voyage this time was a very short one, only occupying one day; and early on the following morning we arrived in sight of Flanders and there brought up at anchor. Very shortly some small vessels came alongside to convey us to the quay at Ostend, where we landed, and after marching about half a mile we came to a canal, where we embarked in large open barges, in which we were towed by horses past Bruges, about twelve miles off Ostend, to Ghent, which at a wide guess might be twice the same distance further. We landed at Ghent and lay there about nine days, while Louis XVIII was staying in the town, he having been obliged to flee from Paris by that old disturber after a short reign of about ten months.

At the end of the nine days the drums beat at midnight, and we arrayed ourselves in marching order as quickly as possible. The landlord of the house where I was staying had got up, and would kindly insist on filling our canteens—that is a capacity of about three pints—with gin, giving us as well some bread and meat each, and warning us to look out, for he knew the French were coming. All having assembled at the rendezvous, orders were given to march on to Brussels immediately. I could not exactly say what the distance was, but it was probably not less than forty miles, taking us two days of hard marching to accomplish it.

CHAPTER 22

Waterloo

On the 17th of June, 1815, we marched through Brussels, amid the joy of the inhabitants, who brought us out all manner of refreshments. I heard some remarks from them to the effect that we were all going to be slaughtered like bullocks, but we only laughed at this, telling them that that was nothing new to us. Some of the younger recruits, however, were terribly downcast and frightened at the idea of fighting, but I have often found that it is these most timid ones who when they come to an actual battle rush forward and get killed first; probably owing to the confused state they are in, while the more disciplined soldiers know better what course to pursue.

From Brussels we marched to about five or six miles out of the town, not far from the village of Waterloo, when our commander sent his aide-de-camp to Lord Wellington for general orders how he was to act, or as to what part of the line we were to fall in at. The orders returned were that we were to stay in our present position till next morning, so that night we crept into any hole we could find, cowsheds, cart-houses, and all kinds of farmstead buildings, for shelter, and I never remember a worse night in all the Peninsular war, for the rain descended in torrents, mixed with fearful thunder and lightning, and seeming to foretell the fate of the following morning, the 18th, which again happened to be Sunday,

The allied army had on the 16th and 17th been attacked by Napoleon's large forces at Ligny and Quatre Bras, but neither side had obtained any great success, beyond thousands being killed on both sides; during the night of the 17th, therefore, firing was continually going on, which I could distinctly hear, in spite of its being considerably drowned by the thunder. All that night was one continued clamour, for thousands of camp-followers were on their retreat to Brussels, fearful of sticking to the army after the Quatre Bras affair. It was indeed a sight, for owing to the rain and continued traffic the roads were almost impassable, and the people were sometimes completely stuck in the mud: and besides these a continual stream of baggage-wagons was kept up through the night.

Early in the morning of the 18th we were again put on the march to join our lines, our position being in the reserve, which included the Fourth and Twenty-Seventh Regiments, together with a body of Brunswickers and Dutch, and formed a line between Merk Braine and Mont St. Jean on the Brussels road. Our regiment took the left of this road, but did not remain there long, for the French were seen in motion, and on their opening fire from their cannon we soon marched up to action in open column.

During this movement a shell from the enemy cut our deputy-sergeant-major in two, and having passed on to take the head off one of my company of grenadiers named William Hooper, exploded in the rear not more than one yard from me, hurling me at least two yards into the air, but fortunately doing me little injury beyond the shaking and carrying a small piece of skin off the side of my face. It was indeed another narrow escape, for it burnt the tail of my sash completely off, and turned the handle of my sword perfectly black. I remember remarking to a sergeant who was standing close by me when I fell, "This is sharp work to begin with, I hope it will end better:" and even this much had unfortunately so frightened one of the young recruits of my company, named Bartram, who had never before been in action and now did not like the curious evolutions of this shell so close to him, that he called out to me and said he must fall out of rank, as he was taken very ill. I could easily see the cause of his illness, so I pushed him into rank again, saying, "Why, Bartram, it's the smell of this little powder that has caused your illness;

there's nothing else the matter with you;" but that physic would not content him at all, and he fell down and would not proceed another inch. I was fearfully put out at this, but was obliged to leave him, or if he had had his due he ought to have been shot. From this time I never saw him again for at least six months, but even then I did not forget him for this affair of cowardice, as I shall have occasion to show hereafter.

The right of our line had been engaged some little time before we were ordered up, and then our position was changed, we having to cross the road and proceed to the right of a farmhouse called La Haye Sainte. Owing to the rain that had been peppering down the whole night and even now had not quite ceased, the fields and roads were in a fearful state of dirt and mud, which tended to retard our progress greatly as well as to tire us. It made it very bad too for the action of cavalry, and even more so for artillery.

About ten o'clock the action of the day began at Hougoumont on our right, and from there it fell on our centre, where we were attacked by a tremendous body of cavalry and infantry. The fire, however, which had been kept up for hours from the enemy's cannon had now to be abated in that quarter, owing to the close unison of the two armies. And from this time onward we endured some heavy work throughout the day, having constantly to be first forming square to receive the repeated attacks of their cavalry, and then line to meet their infantry, charge after charge being made upon us, but with very little success. At the commencement the commanding officer was killed by a musket-shot, but his place was soon filled up.

On our left on the turnpike road was placed a brigade of German cavalry with light horses and men. When Buonaparte's Bodyguards came up they charged these, making fearful havoc amongst their number, they were routed and obliged to retreat, but the Life Guards and Scotch Greys fortunately making their appearance immediately, some close handwork took place, and the Bodyguards at last finding their match, or even more, were in their turn compelled to fall back before the charge of our cavalry, numbers of them being cut to pieces. Still nothing daunted, they formed again, and this time ascended at us; but of the two, they met with a worse reception than before, for we instantly threw ourselves into three squares with our artillery in the centre; and the word having been given not to fire at the men, who wore armour, but at the horses, which was obeyed to the very letter, as soon as they arrived at close quarters we opened a deadly fire, and very few of. them wholly escaped. They managed certainly at first to capture our guns, but they were again recovered by the fire of our three squares; and it was a most laughable sight to see these Guards in their chimney-armour trying to run away after their horses had been shot from under them, being able to make very little progress, and many of them being taken prisoners by those of our light companies who were out skirmishing. I think this quite settled Buonaparte's Bodyguards, for we saw no more of them, they not having expected this signal defeat.

That affair, however, had only passed off a very few minutes before their infantry advanced and we had again to form line ready to meet them. We in our usual style let the infantry get well within our musket-shot before the order was given to fire, so that our volley proved to be of fearful success: and then immediately charging them we gave them a good start back again, but not without a loss on our side as well as on theirs. And no sooner had they disappeared than another charge of cavalry was made, so that we again had to throw ourselves into square on our old ground. These cavalry had no doubt expected to appear amongst us before we could accomplish this, but fortunately they were mistaken, and our persistent fire soon turned them. We did not lose a single inch of ground the whole day, though after these successive charges our numbers were fearfully thinned, and even during the short interval between each charge the enemy's cannon had been doing some mischief among our ranks besides.

The men in their tired state were beginning to despair, but the officers cheered them on continually throughout the day with the cry of "Keep your ground, my men!" It is a mystery to me how it was accomplished, for at last so few were left that there were scarcely enough to form square.

About four o'clock I was ordered to the colours. This, although I was used to warfare as much as any, was a job I did not at all like; but still I went as boldly to work as I could. There had been before me that day fourteen sergeants already killed and wounded while in charge of those colours, with officers in proportion, and the staff and colours were almost cut to pieces. This job will never be blotted from my memory although I am now an old man, I remember it as if it had been yesterday. I had not been there more than a quarter of an hour when a cannon-shot came and took the captain's head clean off. This was again close to me, for my left side was touching the poor captain's right, and I was spattered all over with his blood. One of his company who was close by at the time, cried out, "Hullo, there goes my best friend," which caused a lieutenant, who quickly stepped forward to take his place, to say to the man, "Never mind, I will be as good a friend to you as the captain." The man replied, "I hope not, sir;" the officer not having rightly understood his meaning, the late captain having been particularly hard on him for his dirtiness, giving him extra duty and suchlike as punishment. This man, whose name was Marten, was a notorious character in the regiment, and I was myself tolerably well acquainted with him, for he had once been in my company; but on account of the same thing, dirtiness in his person, he had been transferred to this the fifth company, where neither this poor captain had been able to reform him, try however hard he might. Still he was for all this an excellent soldier in the field.

But now I must get on to the last charge of cavalry, which took place not very long after this. Few as we were, when we saw it coming we formed squares and awaited it Then we poured volley after volley into them, doing fearful execution, and they had to retire at last before the strong dose we administered, not, however, without our losing more men and so becoming even weaker than before. We were dreading another charge, but all the help we got was the cry of "Keep your ground, my men, reinforcements are coming!" Not a bit, however, did they come till the setting sun, in time to pursue our retreating enemy; the Prussians under Marshal Blucher having

145

been detained elsewhere, and although long expected, only being able at this period to make their appearance at last.

I must say here that I cannot think why those charges of cavalry were kept up against our unbroken squares, in spite of their being so constantly sent back. It is murder to send cavalry against disciplined infantry unless they have artillery to act in conjunction with them, in which case they might possibly succeed in routing them if they could take advantage of their falling into confusion, but not otherwise.

We were indeed glad to see the arrival of these Prussians, who now coming up in two columns on our left flank, advanced on the enemy's right. Lord Wellington, who was ever enticing his army on, now came up to our regiment and asked who was in command. On being told it was Captain Brown, he gave the order to advance, which we received with three cheers, and off we set as if renewed with fresh vigour. The attack was now being made by the whole line, together with the Prussians, who had come up fresh and were therefore more than a match for the harassed French. They soon forced the French into a downright retreat by their fire, and the retreat becoming universal, the whole body of the French were thrown into disorder and pursued off the field by Blucher's fresh and untired infantry and cavalry.

We followed them ourselves for about a mile, and then encamped on the enemy's ground; and if ever there was a hungry and tired tribe of men, we were that after that memorable day of the 18th of June. Then the first thing to be thought of was to get a fire and cook some food, which was not so easy, as wood was scarce and what there was was wet through. One of our company, named Rouse, who went out in search of sticks, came across one of the enemy's powder-wagons that we had taken in the battle amongst the rest of the many things, and immediately commenced cutting the cover up for fuel; but his hook coming in contact with a nail or some other piece of iron and striking fire, as a natural consequence the remains of the powder in the wagon exploded and lifted the poor fellow to a considerable height in the air. The most remarkable thing was that he was still alive when he came down and able to speak, though everything had been blown from him except one of his shoes. He was a perfect blackguard, for although he was in a most dangerous state he did not refrain from cursing his eyes, which happened, as it was, to be both gone, and saying what a fool he must have been. He was that night conveyed to Brussels Hospital with the rest of the many wounded, and died in a few days, raving mad.

We succeeded, however, in getting a fire at last, and then as I happened that night to be orderly sergeant to our general I went and reported myself to him. He was at the time sitting on a gun-carriage holding his horse, and when he saw me, said, "That's right, sergeant; I expect two more sergeants directly, but I wish you would meanwhile try and get some corn for my poor horse." Off I went accordingly, and found two bushels or so in a sack which had evidently been left by the enemy, as it was on one of their cannon. When I opened the sack I found to my great surprise that it likewise contained a large ham and two fowls, so I asked the general if he would accept them; he, however, declined, saying he would take the corn, but that I might keep the meat for myself, advising me, however, to keep it out of sight of the Prussians, who were a slippery set of men and very likely to steal it if they saw it.

I prepared the hanger for the pot as quickly as possible, putting cross-sticks over the fire at a sufficient distance to prevent them igniting; but before I had finished doing this a quantity of these same Prussians whom the general had been watching and warned me against passed by, and two of them coming to my fire to light their pipes noticed the ham, and remarked that it looked good. I thought it best to take my sword and immediately cut them off a piece each, and they relieved my fears by going off seemingly quite satisfied. They were evidently on the march following up the French, for the whole night we could hear the distant sound of cannon and musketry from the French and Prussians, Lord Wellington having completely given up the pursuit to Marshal Blucher.

I pretty quickly put my ham in the pot after that, and the two sergeants coming up, I set them to pick the fowls, and these soon going in after the ham, in two hours were pretty well done. About this time I heard a Frenchman groaning under a cannon, where he was lying on a quantity of straw. I thought he was badly wounded, and perhaps as hungry as myself, so I went to him and told him as well as I was able to stop till our supper was cooked, and then I would bring him some; but when it was ready and I had cut off some bread, fowl, and ham, and taken it to the place where I had seen him, he had gone. For one reason I was not sorry, for he left his straw, which made a very good bed for us three sergeants, the ground itself being unpleasantly wet I think perhaps this Frenchman must have been a skulker, or he would not have ventured to escape.

We sat down ourselves, however, and made a very good meal off our ham and poultry, and I can safely say we enjoyed our mess as much as men ever did, for I, for one, had had nothing to eat since early in the morning up to that time. After that, as the general did not want us for anything, we retired to rest on our straw, but I was too tired to go to sleep for a long time, and lay contemplating the scenes of the day. I was merely scratched on the face myself during the whole day, besides being a little shaken by the bursting of the shell I mentioned; but this scratch had been terribly aggravated by a private who had been standing next to me having overprimed his musket, with the consequence that when he fired, my face being so close, the powder flew up and caught my wound, which though only originally a slight one soon made me dance for a time without a fiddle.

Of the general loss on that blood-stained day I am unable to give an exact account, but it must have been enormous on both sides, for three hundred of my regiment alone were missing; and this was not so great a loss as that of some regiments, for the one on our right lost six hundred, chiefly from the continual fire of shot and shell that the French cannon had kept up between the charges. But now there was very little delay; and early next morning we were again put in motion, to prevent our enemy, if possible, from getting any breathing time. The Prussians were at least twelve hours in advance of us, so that we really had not much to fear, but still some doubt was entertained as to whether the enemy would make another stand in their own territory, and in all probability such would have been the case if Blucher had not been pushing so close on their heels. I very much doubt, too, if, had not the Prussians come up when they did, both armies would not have remained on the field of Waterloo, and perhaps have joined battle again in the morning, for the French had been expecting fresh reinforcements after their defeat; but these not arriving and we being increased in numbers, no resource was left them but to retreat.

CHAPTER 23

Advance to Paris

Our march now lay in the direction of Paris, and being made all in the daytime, caused us very little fatigue, as we halted often, besides always encamping or billeting at night. We never fell in with the enemy ourselves, though some few collisions took place between the Prussians and French after this, and likewise some towns were taken by our army; but beyond that our march was generally quiet, and we continued on to within a few miles of, and in sight of Paris, where we remained for a short time, coming up here with our allies the Prussians. They had already opened fire on that city of despotism, which was returned faintly by the enemy, but once the balance is turned, and once a man, however great, is defeated, all seem to forsake him, and he immediately becomes an usurper, as was shown to be true in this Napoleon's case. There is not a doubt that the populace would have held to him if he had been a conqueror, but as it was, the whole city now changed its sentiments from Napoleon to Louis XVIII, who had advanced with us with about fifty of his own guards.

On our approach to the city the inhabitants soon sent a flag of truce for terms, and the firing having ceased on both sides, these were agreed upon, and the city gates were opened. Napoleon Buonaparte had previously flown to the coast to get a ship to America, but not finding one at hand, and fearing that if he stayed on land he might on account of his unpopularity be taken prisoner by his own bloodthirsty people, he went on board and gave himself up to the captain of one of our ships of the line, a seventy-four called the *Bellerophon*. I remember that owing to that event she was very commonly known amongst us as the "Billy Ruffun", and we used to aggravate the people not a little on our march into the city, by singing, "God save Buonaparte, who has fled and given himself up to the Billy Ruffuns." in opposition to their cry of "God save the king;" thousands of them having come out with white cockades in their hats to welcome the king. They even wanted to take the horses out of his carriage and draw him into the city, but Lord Wellington would not allow this, knowing well their changeable disposition, and fearing they might make their king a head shorter by the morning.

The king therefore slept that night at St. Denis, a few miles from Paris, and on the following morning about three thousand men with cannon and cavalry were ordered to convey him into the city, amongst whom was myself. We started at about eleven or twelve o'clock, still not knowing how we should be welcomed, which was the reason for this large force being thought necessary; but as we met with no opposition at the entrance, the bands of each regiment soon struck up, and on proceeding through the streets we found flags from endless windows, and the cry, "God save the king!" resounding everywhere. Our destination was of course the palace, where the king was again placed on his throne, with a strong guard to protect his person.

After this we saw no more of Napoleon's army, nor did we want to much, for most of us had had quite enough of it at Waterloo, and now we found ourselves comfortably quartered at the different barracks throughout the city, where we remained for three months or so scarcely wanting for anything but money. During this time it became my duty to be one of the king's guard two or three times at the palace, which was a splendid place, with fine grounds and a beautiful river running at the back. Nothing of particular note occurred whilst we were staying here, and on leaving it at the end of the time we encamped on Marshal Ney's own property in front of his residence or palace. At that time there could not have been much less than two hundred thousand troops encamped in various parts of and around Paris, and those all of foreign nations: truly a downfall for that noble but despotic city.

In the November of the same year Marshal Ney was brought to justice as a traitor. He was tried by his own country's law, Lord Wellington having nothing to do with the matter, and being found guilty, was shot I believe that he was generally liked by the army he commanded through nearly the whole of the Peninsular campaign.

The Bourbons, on their part, were evidently not liked by the French, for the next heir to Louis XVIII. was assassinated in the streets. His duchess however, very shortly afterwards had a son, and so there was soon another of the family in the way Still these ill-disposed French people could not rest, and the next thing was that two men were caught in the act of undermining the palace, with a view to blow the duchess and her child up. They were tried and sentenced to be guillotined, but the sentence was never carried into effect, as the duchess, in spite of her husband having been killed by the same party, begged their lives of the king, and they were transported for life instead.

During our stay in the environs of Paris the whole army was reviewed by two English Dukes; one of them was the Duke of York, but the other's name I am not able to give, as I never heard. A sham fight was likewise held, in which I should say more powder was thrown away than at Waterloo itself; and I am positive I was quite as tired after it as at Waterloo, for it lasted all day, and a great deal more marching took place than did there, for we were on the move the whole time, while at Waterloo we did not advance or retreat more than a hundred yards during the entire action.

The inhabitants kept up a continual market at the rear of our camp, which was always guarded by sentries to prevent plunder, and so we could always easily obtain supplies of every description. While we were lying there several of the wounded who had recovered rejoined the army from Brussels, and with some of these Bartram made his appearance, the man whom I mentioned as having smelt powder at the beginning of the 18th of

June, and having so cowardly fallen out of his rank. As soon as I saw him I put him in the rear-guard as a prisoner, and reported him, as it was my duty to do, to the captain of my company. Next day a court-martial was ordered, I being the chief but not the only evidence against him, and being sentenced to three hundred lashes as a punishment for absenting himself from the field of action, he was tied up and received every lash.

This may seem to some a hard case, three hundred lashes for absenting himself, but it must be remembered that had there been many like this man, for I cannot call him a soldier, that day would most decidedly have ended in favour of the French. When taken down he was sent to hospital for three weeks and then came back to us, but even then he was not quite free, for I had orders from the captain to examine his kit to see if everything was complete, and I found his knapsack completely empty. I then searched his pouch and found all his ammunition gone. I was not much surprised at this, knowing that he did not like the smell of powder; but I reported these circumstances to the captain, who ordered him back to the rearguard as a prisoner again; and the next day another court-martial was held on him for making away with his kit, and he was sentenced to three hundred more lashes, of which strange to say he received every one without crying out. He seemed to be a man without any feeling, for it may be pretty well taken for granted that the drummers did not fail in their duty towards such a man as this, for there is no one they feel more strongly against than a coward.

He was then sent for three weeks more to the hospital, and at the end of the time again joined; but the poor fellow must after that have been very miserable, for all his comrades shunned his society and would scarcely speak to him at all: and not only that, but having had a new kit and sixty rounds of ball-cartridge supplied to him, he had sixpence a day stopped out of his money till they were paid for, his pay being only thirteen pence a day, so that after another sixpence had been stopped for his food he had only one penny per day to take. I need hardly say that he was consequently always without money, and at last we missed him for two or three days, after which he returned, having again lost his kit We found he had been into Paris and sold it for those two or three days' maintenance, so he was again sent to the rear-guard and reported, again court-martialed and sentenced to three hundred lashes, and again received the whole to the very letter and sent to hospital for the same time. When he again rejoined he went on better for a while, but on our regiment afterwards getting to Scotland he transgressed and was flogged for a fourth time, and when he came out of hospital the colonel ordered his coat to be turned, and a large sheet of paper to be pinned on it with the words, "This is a coward, a very bad soldier, and one who has been whipped four times;" and he was then drummed out of the barracks, and I never saw anything of him again, which I was not sorry for, as he gave me more trouble than all the rest of my men put together.

The reason of our stay in and about Paris so long was to see Louis XVIII. thoroughly fixed again and in power on his throne. The armies being now moved into winter quarters chiefly in cantonments, our brigade took its route to St. Germains, which lies ten or twelve miles to the north-west of Paris on the River Seine, where we remained quartered a few months.

It was owing to this long stay, and my happening to see a young woman who gained my affections, that it fell out that I first then thought of marriage. For outside the barrack-gate where we were quartered was a movable stall, which was spread out in the day with fruit, spirits, tobacco, snuff, &c, and was cleared away at night This was kept by the woman whom I afterwards made my wife. Her father was a gardener in business for himself, and this was the way in which he disposed of most of his goods. My first introduction was through my going to purchase a few articles that I wanted from her, and it very shortly became a general thing for me to dispose of the chief of such time as I had to spare at the stall, and thus the attachment was formed of which I am happy to say I never afterwards repented.

I happened to be at the stall one day when I saw a soldier of the Twenty-Seventh Regiment, which was stationed at the barracks as well as ours, deliberately take half a pound of tobacco which was already tied up off the stall and attempt to get off with it. But that didn't suit me, so I pursued and overtook him, and delivered him over to his own regiment to dispose of as they thought best after I had told them the circumstances. I told them too that I didn't wish to prosecute him myself, so I never heard anything more of him. I took the tobacco, however, back to my intended, who of course was pleased, as what young woman would not have been under the circumstances we were then in? And so our courtship went on; but for a very little while, for once we were enamoured of one another we were not long in making things all square for our union.

I made my intentions known to my captain, who I knew would not object, and he signed my paper to take to the colonel, whose permission I had next to get. The colonel could not understand at first my marrying a Frenchwoman, but he nevertheless consented, saying that she would do to teach the soldiers French, but that he advised me to wait till I got to England. But having got the grant, it was a question of now or never for me, so I made arrangements with the army chaplain, who fixed the time and we were duly united. It cost us nothing, for neither the parson nor clerk looked for any fee, neither were we troubled with any wedding-cake, but simply took ourselves off for a day's merrymaking.

My wife's maiden name had been Marie Louise Claire, but owing to Buonaparte's first wife having been Marie Louise too, she had been compelled to drop that name and assume that of Clotilde; a proclamation having been made that no one should be called Marie Louise but the Empress, and so by that vain freak of Buonaparte's all in France who were called Marie Louise had to change their names.

Of course before marrying her I had explained to my wife the course of life she would have to put up with, and that at any moment we might have to proceed from her native place, and even might be recalled to England, but she did not mind the prospect of all this. And at length the time arrived that we had to go, for orders were, given, and that on very short notice, that we were to prepare to resume our march. A farewell had then to be taken of her parents, whom we expected never to behold again, and this cast a slight shadow for a time over my wife's countenance, but it quickly passed away within the next few succeeding days.

Chapter 24

The March to Calais

From St Germain we proceeded to Cambray. We were bil-leted at a village near Cambray called Aresne, where we had very good quarters and found the people particularly kind, and after remaining there a short time we were moved to a neighbouring village, where we got equally good quarters.

But here another of those unpleasant things happened which often have to occur that proper discipline and justice may be kept up. A part of the Twenty-Seventh Regiment was billeted at a village near where we were situated, most of whom were I believe Irish; and two of the more ruffianly, knowing that a farmer who lived close by had gone to market, and would probably return laden with the value of the goods he had sold, laid wait for him with the intention of robbing him; and having met him, they fell upon him and left him in a corn-field evidently for dead, first stripping him of everything valuable about his person. There the man lay till his friends becoming uneasy at his long absence a search was made and he was tracked to his mournful bed. He was not dead when found, and so was conveyed to his house and properly attended to by a doctor, and at the end of a week he was able to give an account of the ill-treatment he said he had received at the hands of two soldiers who were quartered in the village occupied by the Twenty-Seventh Regiment. One of the officers was consequently informed of the occurrence, and immediately went to the farmer to learn the rights of the story. The man could not tell the amount of money that had been taken from him, but he said he could recognize the men again. As soon, therefore, as he was able to walk, the officer took him down the ranks of his regiment, and certainly he proved to be correct about recognizing them, for he immediately picked out two men who were found to have been out at the time described. They were conveyed as prisoners to the guard-room, and reported to the general, who immediately ordered a court-martial, and, accepting the evidence of their sergeant, who pronounced them to be as often tipsy as not, found them guilty, and they were sentenced to be hanged. The sentence was, however, first sent to be approved of by Lord Wellington, who sanctioned it and returned it; and the execution was accordingly ordered to be carried out.

The men were allowed a week to prepare themselves for their awful doom, and at the end of that time the brigade was called together to take warning from their unhappy fate. It was on a Monday morning that we formed square round the gallows which had been erected for the occasion; and all being ready, the men were brought under the gallows in a spring-wagon guarded by a sergeant and twelve men of their own regiment, one of which latter having adjusted the ropes, the chaplain read the service. Then the question usual in these cases was put, but all they had to say was that they were both guilty and hoped this would be a warning to their comrades. The chaplain then left them, and on the wagon being moved along they were left dancing on nothing. The poor fellows were not long in expiring, but they were left one hour before they were cut down, during which time we had to retain our post, and at the end of it each regiment retired solemnly to its own quarters, leaving a company of the men's own regiment to bury them.

During the brigade's stay near Cambray an order was received that a captain and five sergeants from each regiment should be sent to Valenciennes to learn the sword exercise; so Captain Barnard of my own company was chosen, and amongst the five of our sergeants myself. We started accordingly to Valenciennes, which was about twenty-five or thirty miles from Cambray, and remained there six weeks till we got sick enough of the sword exercise, having six hours a day of it for the whole six weeks except on Sundays. At the end of that time we again joined our regiment, which had been ordered to return immediately to Scotland.

The day after our arrival the regiment was put on the march for Calais. We were quartered in cantonments every night, and at one of our sleeping-places I met a Jew, and having a silver watch to dispose of, I asked him what he would give me for it. He replied fifteen francs and a silk dress, which I took, and when we arrived at Calais we changed the French money into English; but since I had left my own country the coinage had been altered, which bothered me a little at first sight, and certainly did not bring me any gain. We lay in Calais two nights, where I and my wife got very comfortable quarters. I may as well say here that she had borne the marches quite as well as I did, if not in some cases better.

Three colliers had been contracted with to convey our regiment to Scotland, and from the appearance of the vessels themselves, I very much doubted, if bad weather should set in, that we should ever reach Leith, the port we set sail for, they being the rickettiest old watertubs I ever saw. Leith was supposed to be three days' sail from Calais with a fair wind, but we had a foul one nearly the whole time, and we were seven weeks on the voyage, having to put in at Bridlington in Yorkshire to wait for this fair wind. My wife, who had never before seen salt water, was at first ill and found the whole voyage terribly long and tedious, but to me, who had long since learnt not to be troubled with trifles, it mattered not weather or no, and I was by this time thoroughly used too to long voyages by water after my American trips.

Our stay at Bridlington lasted three weeks. The first night we were there, the mayor invited the officers to dine with him, and sent a quart of beer on board for each man, and half that quantity for each woman. During our stay here too, we were allowed to go on shore in the day but obliged to be on board by nine o'clock at night The inhabitants were particularly kind to us, amongst other things offering our women their houses to wash their clothes in, which offer many accepted. And here I at last got a chance to get rid of my silk dress, which was a thing that my wife hardly required while travelling about, and I had been trying to dispose of it ever since I obtained it I used to visit a public-house in the neighbourhood where I noticed the daughter of the place, a fine-looking girl, used to sport her silk dress, so I sold her mine for fifty shillings and a gallon of beer, which latter I gave to her customers.

At last the favouring breeze sprang up, and we again attempted to proceed on our voyage. We were a whole day getting opposite Shields, and a pilot was signalled for, but before he arrived we were again obliged to fall back to Bridlington, which took us but nine hours to do, during the whole of which time the vessel rolled fearfully, and the women especially began to despair. Our stay lasted for ten days this time, and then we proceeded again to Shields, where we lay for a week, being likewise allowed to go on shore there. Our walks on shore sometimes extended to the coal-mines, and we also went over the glass-manufactories, which last amused my wife more than anything. The workmen made her a smelling-bottle and me several pipes and a walking-stick of glass, for us to see the process.

From Shields we proceeded to Leith, and landed, and all our baggage being examined at the customs-house, I thought what a capital thing it was that I had sold my dress. That night we remained in Leith, and on the following morning were ordered to march to Glasgow, which we reached on the third day.

CHAPTER 25

The New Set of Colours

The barracks at Glasgow we found to be comfortable; and after lying there about three months, the winter of 1817 set in, and furloughs were granted for two months to a part of the regiment. As I had a wife with me and my home was so far away, I gave my furlough to a fellow-sergeant that he might go to Ireland; but I wrote home and told them I had arrived in England, and very soon received an answer back from my mother to say my father was ill, and if I did not come then, perhaps I should never see him again. I consulted my wife as to the journey, and she readily consented to come with me, so I made up my mind to try for another furlough. I accordingly took the old lady's letter to the captain, who said, "Well, sergeant, there are so many gone that I don't know whether the colonel will let you, but we will ask him;" so we went to him, and on hearing the nature of my case he readily consented to allow me, six weeks, and signed my furlough. He likewise advanced me one shilling per day for the six weeks, and as I had lately received my Waterloo prize-money which was twenty pounds, I started off with that, having previously bought some requisites in clothing and a watch, the sort of things that make one feel a little more respectable.

My intentions were to proceed to Leith to get a vessel bound for London, and then to walk the remaining distance, which is upwards of a hundred miles. The first day's march brought us twenty miles nearer Leith, and we accomplished the remaining part on the following day; and the next morning I went in search of a vessel, and finding a Leith trader bound for London,

I took passage in her for two, the captain charging two guineas and a half including board. We were to sail next day, and true to time we started, but owing to a heavy wind we were obliged to run in and anchor at Berwick. While there a revenue cutter which was cruising about came too close to us and knocked our little vessel's bowsprit off, disabling her for three days; but when all was put right we again set sail, and having a fair wind soon arrived in the London Docks.

It being night we remained on board till the following morning, when, after having had our breakfast, we started for Piccadilly, which we found after a good deal of inquiry. A hackney cab then drove up to us and the driver wanted to know where we were going, and on our telling him and asking him the way, he said he would put us into the right road for two shillings. I offered him eighteen pence, but he would not take that, so we got him to show us the way and proceeded on walking. We had not got farther than Hyde Park Corner, however, than we were again overtaken by the same cab, and the man stopped and said that he thought he could take us for the money now. He had one gentleman, an Englishman, inside already, but evidently the sharp fellow was looking out for a double fare; so he asked this gentleman if we might get inside as we were going in the same direction. He politely and readily consented, and we were forked in by cabby, who then shot off as if the whole road was his own.

I was under the necessity of talking French to my wife, as she could not understand English, which of course I made known to the gentleman, who replied that he knew a little of that language himself. Then, noticing my Waterloo medal on my breast, he said, "I see you have been in the battle of Waterloo, sergeant?"

"Yes," I replied, "and in many other battles besides Waterloo;" and so a conversation ensued and we soon became quite friends. He wished to know where I was bound for, and when I told him, he politely asked me to spend a week at his house on the way, saying I should not want for anything; but I told him the reason of my hurry, thanking him for his kindness, and his stage having expired at this period he got out But he would insist on giving my wife five shillings and paying our fare: we then shook hands heartily and parted, he wishing us good-speed on our journey.

After that we walked on some distance till we came to a village where we found the Salisbury road-wagon put up, and being very hungry we entered a public-house and had some tea, and waited there till ten o'clock. I was enjoying myself over my tobacco, when at nightfall some ten or twelve customers came in and I spun them a pretty good yarn, making them shake with laughter; but what amused them most, though it annoyed my wife a little to see them laugh at what she could not understand, was to hear me and her talk French together. At ten o'clock the party broke up and I called for my bill, which was fourpence for a glass of gin for myself and eight-pence for the boiling water for our tea, which was much to my surprise, as we had found our own food, tea, and sugar. I asked the landlady if it was not a mistake, and when she said no, I told her I wished she and her charges were at the other side of the moon. However, I paid her, though I gave her to understand that if we had been in the enemy's country we should have got our boiling water for nothing.

We then joined the road-wagon, which was to start for Salisbury at midnight I spoke to the wagoner, who agreed to take us for two shillings and told us we could get in at once, so, as we were very tired, we did so, and lying down, soon fell fast asleep; and when we awoke we found ourselves jogging on towards Salisbury, where we arrived late the next night. I paid the man his well-earned two shillings, besides which I had treated him to sundry refreshments on the way; and we remained at Salisbury for the rest of the night, starting early on the following morning for Blandford. We marched seven miles before breakfast, and after it did not halt again till we got to Blandford, where stayed the night, and next morning, which was Sunday, proceeded on towards my native village, which is about eight miles from Blandford.

We arrived there during church service in the morning, and passing through the churchyard as a near cut, went up the village, inquiring at several houses where John Lawrence, my father, lived. I found it was at the same house where I was born, but strange to say I did not at all hurry myself to get there. I had found from the neighbours that he was still living and much better, so I was at ease on that point.

At last, however, I strolled into a house, the owner of which I well knew before I entered on my rambling life, but who was now turned into an old woman, and I asked her the same question that I had already put to others in the village, saying that I had seen my parents' son, and had got a message for them. But woman's piercing eyes are not so easily deceived, and she recognized me as a Lawrence, though she did not know whether it was William or John. I certified as to that much, and she immediately ran off to bring my sister. As may be well imagined in a country place like that, we two strangers, one of us dressed as a soldier, and our entering so many houses, had already set the place all of a stir to know who we were, and now directly it was found out, it was telegraphed all through the village. Before I could get to my own door my sister was upon me, and did try to kiss me, certainly, but I had not shaved since I left Scotland, and now I had a long thick beard and moustache, so that the attempt was almost a fruitless task. She cried out, "Come in; why don't you shave?" so I asked her if there was any barber handy. "No," she replied," but I'll shave you, for I always do father," so in I went. My father and mother were still out at church. My wife meanwhile could hardly make out these scenes that were transpiring, not seeming to dare to interrupt the proceedings with one French word to me; and my sister not having yet thought to ask me who this mysterious woman was, she followed me indoors without any questioning and like myself sat down. I pulled off my knapsack, and the shaving-tackle was brought out; but it put me so much in mind of the ceremony with the iron hoop when we crossed the Line that I became impatient, and opening my knapsack took out my own razor and finished myself.

By this time church was over, and putting my head out of the door I beheld my brother, who could scarcely speak to me owing to his feelings. I found both my father and mother had stopped to take the sacrament, but when it was over I suddenly saw the old lady who had got scent of the matter coming along like a spread-eagle with the same old black bonnet and red cloak on that she had when I left her. I went to meet her, but she was so overcome with emotion that I had to lean her up against the house to prevent her falling, and then I proceeded on to the old man, who was quite infirm and hobbling along behind on two sticks, and I need hardly say that he behaved worse than any of them at my strange and sudden appearance. I led him in and got him with difficulty to a chair. None of us then spoke for a long time, but at last the old man gave utterance to, "My child, I did not expect to see you again" It was indeed sixteen long years since I had left them at Dorchester.

My wife, though of course she could not understand a word, was much affected by this scene. I now began to throw a word or two to her occasionally in her own language, which surprised them a good deal, and no less were they astonished when I told them she was my wife. No doubt she felt queer with all strangers round her and in a foreign land, which to her was like a new world, but by the evening we were all reconciled to each other; and by that time too we had dozens of friends and neighbours in to see us. My wife particularly wished to know what all these people wanted, as so many could not be all relations, so I told her that they had chiefly come to see her, as they had never seen a Frenchwoman before; but of course she would not believe this piece of flattery.

I then thought of wetting the subject a little, but there was no public-house in the village, the nearest being at Piddletown about three miles off. However, I got one of my brothers to go even that distance, and he having brought back four gallons, we made ourselves comfortable till ten o'clock, when we retired to rest in the same room that I had slept in eighteen years before.

After a good night's rest we rose early and found all recovering themselves, except perhaps the old lady, who had not yet done piping. After breakfast I took a walk round the village and fell in with the clergyman of the place, who would insist, on taking me to his house and giving me some ale; and when he had once got me there, he kept me for at least an hour, the chief topics we talked about being the war and the religion of the countries I had been in. I was glad enough to get away from there, but I had to spend the whole of that day in visiting the people of the village; and the next day I had to occupy still worse, for my mother brought out every letter sent by me during my absence from the first to the last, and made me listen to them being read, which by the time night came on had almost sent me crazy. I advised her to burn the lot, but that only made her put them back in their place again, saying, "Never, William, so long as I live."

We passed the next two days visiting such of my brothers arid sisters as lived more near, and then as I could not rest in one place for long, on the third morning I set out with my wife for Corfe Mullen, about twelve miles off, to see another brother who was a farm-labourer there. After some few inquiries for George Lawrence I found out his house, and was answered at the door by his wife, who of course had no knowledge who I was, though I had known her before her marriage. She did not ask me in, but pointed out a barn, where she said I would find George. I went over and he was there threshing, so I said, "Well, friend, do you thresh by the day or the quarter?" He answered, "By the quarter, but I cannot do much of it" He stared at me, for I had on my regimentals, but I did not yet make myself known. Then I asked him if there was a public-house handy. He said there was one just below, so I told him that if he would go there with me I would treat him, as his must be hard work, and he thanked me and led the way.

I ordered some beer and tobacco with pipes, and after that took off my shako which I could not bear any longer, and he immediately recognized me as his brother William. We then went to his home to be introduced to his wife, and we stayed there two days, after which we returned to Bryant's Piddle and remained with the old people for the rest of the eighteen days I had allotted for our stay out of the six weeks; the going and returning taking away above half our furlough. The morning we left was quite as bad as the morning of my appearance, my wife, who had got used to the old people, being quite as loud as any of them; till at last being sick of the whole affair I buckled on my knapsack, and bidding them good-bye, as quickly as possible took myself off, leaving my wife to follow with my brother to Dorchester, he having volunteered to go with us as far as that.

I had planned out a different way for my journey back, intending to find a ship at Bristol to take us to Scotland and with this view I proceeded westwards, parting from my brother at Dorchester. We found a public-house by the roadside a little way from Dorchester, and after stopping there for the night, continued through Sherborne towards Bristol. On the way we fell in with one of the light company of my regiment, called Warren, who said he was going to London to get a ship back to Scotland; but when I told him of my way of getting there, he immediately said he would go with us; only he had got no money, and hoped I would lend him some. I declined doing this as I had very little myself, but I told him that if he liked to come and live as we did, I would pay for his food and lodging till we got to the regiment, to which he consented and we marched on together.

But when we got to Bristol we found there was no ship going to Scotland, so my wife who was an excellent walker proposed going all the way by road; and accordingly on the following day we started, doing generally two stages a day, through Gloucester, Worcester, Manchester, and Carlisle, and so to Glasgow, a long and tedious march. Our companion, who was anything but a pleasant one, left us at Manchester. We returned to the barracks just one day before my time expired, with only twopence-halfpenny in my pocket and having had to sell my watch for subsistence on the way. After reporting myself, however, I drew my remaining ten pence per day for the six weeks, a penny being deducted from my pay per day for small beer, which was not allowed while I was away. Soon after our arrival at the barracks my wife became very ill owing to having been frostbitten during the march, and remained so for upwards of a week.

We had not been here very long before General Sir George Osborne, the head colonel of our regiment, came expressly to review us; he being a very old man, and not having seen his regiment for some years. After going through our facings, we were arranged in a square, into which the old gentleman entered and presented us with a new stand of colours, then he addressed us as he said for the last time, and hoped his colours would endure as well as our old ones had and be crowned with an equal amount of victory. On them were engraved in gilt letters, *The Peninsula* and *Waterloo* He then took a farewell leave of his regiment, as he doubted if he would ever see it again, and we returned triumphant with our new colours to the barracks. But I may as well add here that every man received sixpence from the old colonel to drink his health.

Chapter 26

Studland

Very shortly after this the army was reduced, and our regiment was made six hundred instead of a thousand strong. First all the old and disabled were discharged, and then lots were cast for the remainder, and the lot falling on me amongst the sergeants, at the end of about a month I and nine others were ordered to Chatham. We marched to Leith, where we embarked on the Leith packet, and after some very rough weather landed at Gravesend and proceeded to Chatham, remaining there six weeks while we were waiting to pass the board. Then we reembarked on a small craft at Gravesend and went up the river to the Tower of London, whence we marched to Chelsea Hospital. The next morning, after we had been examined by the doctor, we were called up before the board one at a time. I was asked my age and time of service, and one of the gentlemen called out "Seven!" but the doctor immediately said "Nine!" as I had a wound in my knee; they evidently meaning that I should have ninepence a day as my pension, as that was what was settled on me for life. I then went to the office, where I received my expenses to Dorchester, to the amount of one and ten-pence for myself, and three-halfpence for my wife for every ten miles; and with that we started off for Bryant's Piddle again, and walked every step of the way, not, however, meeting any such kind gentleman this time as we had on our last route to the same place.

When we arrived we found them all as well as when we had left, but I did not want to stay there long, so on the following morning I took leave of them and proceeded with my wife to

Studland, the place where I had been apprenticed, as I claimed that rightly as my parish. I put up at the public-house till I could procure a house and some furniture, which last took me about a week, and then my next undertaking was to try for work, for it may well be imagined that my wife and I could hardly live on my pension of ninepence a day. I soon obtained employment on a farm close by, for which I received ten shillings a week. I was only in the capacity of a labourer, and it certainly seemed to come very hard at first, but I soon got used to it, and I worked for this master for nine months. He had been formerly a captain in the navy, and I found him very sharp but very just

My reason for leaving him was a sudden call I received to again join the army. I started on the fifth of November, 1819: I was ordered to Plymouth, where I joined the Third Veteran Battalion, which was about a thousand strong at the time, and from Plymouth we went on to Ireland, where we landed at the Cove of Cork and marched through Cork to Fermoy. We went on next day to Templemore, which took us two or three days, and after staying there about a month, three companies of the regiment, myself being one of the number, were ordered to Tralee in county Kerry. When we arrived at Tralee a detachment of a lieutenant, myself, a corporal, and seventeen men were ordered next day to go to Dingle, which is situated on a large tongue of land, and here we were again stationed in barracks for about a year, our principal duty being to guard the coast against the smuggling that was at that time being carried on to a very great extent.

We were chiefly under the command of the coastguard captain, whose name was Collis. It was astonishing to see the many manoeuvres which the inhabitants practised in this art of smuggling. I remember once being called out by the captain to search a house that he had received information about as containing a quantity of smuggled tobacco. I went with twelve men and the captain to the house, and at the door we were met by three ruffianly-looking Irishmen, whose conversation we could not understand at all. however, we passed on and searched the house, at one end of which were standing three cows, which did not seem to me at the time to be very homely guests. At first we could find nothing, so we were proceeding to search the outside, when I saw the three men laughing. Not feeling at all satisfied I turned the cows out and looked under the litter, where I discovered a trap-door, under which when I had opened it I found a flight of steps leading into a cellar, which contained upwards of twenty bales of tobacco. This made the men's countenances change instantaneously. We brought this up, but still not being content we searched farther into the garden, and finding that ground had lately been moved, we disturbed it again and turned up about twelve bales more that were concealed there. These we conveyed in press-carts to the captain's house, and received a good supper for our services and extra pay, mine amounting to half a crown and the privates' less in proportion. On another occasion, when we were again out on the search, we passed what we thought was a funeral, to which we presented arms, but which we afterwards found was nothing but smuggled tobacco put into a box of the shape of a coffin with a pall over, and in this way conveyed into security. Such and similar transactions were frequent during our stay here, the inhabitants being of the very wildest sort Once even a cotton-ship drove ashore, and we had the greatest difficulty in keeping them from plundering it.

At last, however, we were ordered back to Plymouth, so had to march to Waterford Harbour, whither after joining our other companions at Tralee we proceeded, and embarking on board a transport, arrived at Plymouth about June in the year 1821. Thus finally ended my military career, which had lasted seventeen years and seven months, the greater part of the time having been spent on active service. I was discharged on the same pension as before of ninepence a day, that having been stopped during my stay in the Third Veteran Battalion.

From Plymouth I and my wife marched back to Studland, where we took a house, and my master immediately took me back to work. I drifted about, however, between one or two trades, and finally took a little public-house, where I and my wife lived pretty prosperously till she died. I began to feel rather unwell, too, and thought it best to give up working and the public-house so I wrote to the authorities at Chelsea, and obtained through the influence of a kind gentleman an addition of three-pence a day to my pension, making a shilling in all, and with that I am now living in a house that was bequeathed to me for as long as I live by my late master, as comfortably as these circumstances and the interposition of a few friends can make me.

And to conclude I may add that I have striven here as well as my faculties will allow, though I know that is imperfectly, to sum up as it were in a small compass, so that they can be read over in a few hours by the residing populace, the leading scenes of my life, coupled as they have been with the various campaigns I served in; and though I am sorry that I cannot give the reader fuller details of the Peninsula and Waterloo, yet I think that if any even of my comrades themselves who went through the same campaigns, were to take up my work to examine it, they could not say that such information as I have been able to give has been wrong.

LEONAUR

ALSO FROM LEONAUR
AVAILABLE IN SOFTCOVER OR HARDCOVER WITH DUST JACKET

THE JENA CAMPAIGN: 1806 *by F. N. Maude*—The Twin Battles of Jena & Auerstadt Between Napoleon's French and the Prussian Army.

PRIVATE O'NEIL *by Charles O'Neil*—The recollections of an Irish Rogue of H. M. 28th Regt.—The Slashers— during the Peninsula & Waterloo campaigns of the Napoleonic wars.

ROYAL HIGHLANDER *by James Anton*—A soldier of H.M 42nd (Royal) Highlanders during the Peninsular, South of France & Waterloo Campaigns of the Napoleonic Wars.

CAPTAIN BLAZE *by Elzéar Blaze*—Elzéar Blaze recounts his life and experiences in Napoleon's army in a well written, articulate and companionable style.

LEJEUNE VOLUME 1 *by Louis-François Lejeune*—The Napoleonic Wars through the Experiences of an Officer on Berthier's Staff.

LEJEUNE VOLUME 2 *by Louis-François Lejeune*—The Napoleonic Wars through the Experiences of an Officer on Berthier's Staff.

FUSILIER COOPER *by John S. Cooper*—Experiences in the 7th (Royal) Fusiliers During the Peninsular Campaign of the Napoleonic Wars and the American Campaign to New Orleans.

CAPTAIN COIGNET *by Jean-Roch Coignet*—A Soldier of Napoleon's Imperial Guard from the Italian Campaign to Russia and Waterloo.

FIGHTING NAPOLEON'S EMPIRE *by Joseph Anderson*—The Campaigns of a British Infantryman in Italy, Egypt, the Peninsular & the West Indies During the Napoleonic Wars.

CHASSEUR BARRES *by Jean-Baptiste Barres*—The experiences of a French Infantryman of the Imperial Guard at Austerlitz, Jena, Eylau, Friedland, in the Peninsular, Lutzen, Bautzen, Zinnwald and Hanau during the Napoleonic Wars.

MARINES TO 95TH (RIFLES) *by Thomas Fernyhough*—The military experiences of Robert Fernyhough during the Napoleonic Wars.

HUSSAR ROCCA *by Albert Jean Michel de Rocca*—A French cavalry officer's experiences of the Napoleonic Wars and his views on the Peninsular Campaigns against the Spanish, British And Guerilla Armies.

SERGEANT BOURGOGNE *by Adrien Bourgogne*—With Napoleon's Imperial Guard in the Russian Campaign and on the Retreat from Moscow 1812 - 13.

LEONAUR

ALSO FROM LEONAUR
AVAILABLE IN SOFTCOVER OR HARDCOVER WITH DUST JACKET

CAPTAIN OF THE 95th (Rifles) *by Jonathan Leach*—An officer of Wellington's Sharpshooters during the Peninsular, South of France and Waterloo Campaigns of the Napoleonic Wars.

BUGLER AND OFFICER OF THE RIFLES *by William Green & Harry Smith* With the 95th (Rifles) during the Peninsular & Waterloo Campaigns of the Napoleonic Wars

BAYONETS, BUGLES AND BONNETS *by James 'Thomas' Todd*—Experiences of hard soldiering with the 71st Foot - the Highland Light Infantry - through many battles of the Napoleonic wars including the Peninsular & Waterloo Campaigns

THE ADVENTURES OF A LIGHT DRAGOON *by George Farmer & G.R. Gleig*—A cavalryman during the Peninsular & Waterloo Campaigns, in captivity & at the siege of Bhurtpore, India

THE COMPLEAT RIFLEMAN HARRIS *by Benjamin Harris as told to & transcribed by Captain Henry Curling*—The adventures of a soldier of the 95th (Rifles) during the Peninsular Campaign of the Napoleonic Wars

WITH WELLINGTON'S LIGHT CAVALRY *by William Tomkinson*—The Experiences of an officer of the 16th Light Dragoons in the Peninsular and Waterloo campaigns of the Napoleonic Wars.

SURTEES OF THE RIFLES *by William Surtees*—A Soldier of the 95th (Rifles) in the Peninsular campaign of the Napoleonic Wars.

ENSIGN BELL IN THE PENINSULAR WAR *by George Bell*—The Experiences of a young British Soldier of the 34th Regiment 'The Cumberland Gentlemen' in the Napoleonic wars.

WITH THE LIGHT DIVISION *by John H. Cooke*—The Experiences of an Officer of the 43rd Light Infantry in the Peninsula and South of France During the Napoleonic Wars

NAPOLEON'S IMPERIAL GUARD: FROM MARENGO TO WATERLOO by *J. T. Headley*—This is the story of Napoleon's Imperial Guard from the bearskin caps of the grenadiers to the flamboyance of their mounted chasseurs, their principal characters and the men who commanded them.

BATTLES & SIEGES OF THE PENINSULAR WAR *by W. H. Fitchett*—Corunna, Busaco, Albuera, Ciudad Rodrigo, Badajos, Salamanca, San Sebastian & Others

AVAILABLE ONLINE AT
www.leonaur.com
AND OTHER GOOD BOOK STORES

NAP-1